Amaranth (p. 46)

Plantain (p. 51)

Chickweed (p. 53)

Purslane (p. 56)

Mulberry (p. 75)

Lilly pilly (p. 81)

Pink peppercorn or
peppercorn tree (p. 86)

Wild olives: African
and European (p. 90)

Chapter 03
—
Sea

P. 110

Golden kelp (p. 119)

Sea lettuce (p. 123)

Deadman's fingers (p. 127)

Eat

Weeds

ACKNOWLEDGEMENT OF COUNTRY

Here in Australia, we all stand on the shoulders of the oldest culture on Earth.

I pay respect to the Traditional Owners and the stories embedded in the landscape around us.

I acknowledge that Aboriginal and Torres Strait Islander peoples have an unbroken, never-ceded connection and guardianship obligation to this land. The stories that articulate this connection are the stories of the land, and it is through these narratives that law, lore and responsibilities are preserved and passed on from generation to generation.

I am constantly inspired and filled with awe by the knowledge that surrounds me, stories older than memory. Stories that arc back to a time before language, when the sound of the wind through the trees blended with the calls of birds and the whisper of shifting sands to create songs and myths that would guide and frame Aboriginal and Torres Strait Islander cultures through tens of thousands of years.

Wherever I am in Australia, and especially on Country I now consider to be my home, I am always deeply aware of being on Aboriginal land. Most of my experiences and learning documented here have been on Darug, Guringai, Dharawal, Gandangara, Yuin and Wiradjuri Country.

I pay respect to those peoples and the contemporary communities who will always be the traditional custodians of their lands. I pay respect to their Elders and story keepers and offer my efforts in upholding the irrefutable rights and sovereignty of the original custodians of Country.

The vast majority of the plants and stories that I present in this book are exotic, having been imported or infiltrated into this continent since European colonisation 250 years ago. I offer stories entrusted to me in my traditional language, Piedmontese, along with those I have learnt from other custodians from around the world who are now living in Australia.

I have sought permission from original custodians for every single story that I am sharing in this book.

I hope for a society where Indigenous people and cultures are heard, n and respected, and express my commitment to work towards such a society.

Always was, always will be, Aboriginal land.

NOTE ON GEOGRAPHY

Growing up in northern Italy, gathering wild plants was a task my mother would give me to educate me. Actively familiarising myself with the local ecology – watching, listening, tasting – through a process of trial and error, I gradually acquired my 'plant eyes'. Rather than learning to see 'weeds', I was teaching myself to recognise nutritious, edible sources of sustenance and healing, gifted to us by nature.

I have applied my experience growing up in northern Italy to my new home in Australia and this knowledge can be applied even more generally. The plants in this book are mostly universally found and this book is for anyone who wants to know more about our ecology and our role in it. While the book has Australian origins and strong Australian topographies, the theories and philosophies within are entirely global.

Eat

A field guide to foraging:
how to identify, harvest,
eat and use wild plants.

Diego Bonetto

Weeds

Contents

Foreword by
Costa Georgiadis

Diego Bonetto is as mongrel and resilient as the plants that he celebrates. He possesses all of the traits and characteristics that make weeds such an ever-present everyday phenomenon. His book engages the everywhere with the everybody. The plants he showcases and introduces are a gift that is only limited by our vocabulary and communication skills. Diego speaks the language of wild nature. It is part of the very DNA he grew up with on the land, and this book is an invitation to observe the world around us with a whole new set of goggles.

His energy and storytelling capacity are as indefatigable as the weeds that he traces, harvests and shares at the table as edibles or medicinals. He is in all honesty a weed: vibrant, adaptable, capable and filled with an abundance of energy to share. His love of their story will set you off on a journey that will open up a landscape of new views, outlooks, tastes, flavours and connections to the very blueprint and operating system of our plants. His expert guidance is at the core of this guidebook. Hold on for the ride.

Disclaimer

Every effort has been made to provide accurate information about the plants in this book and safe ways to ingest them. However, each forager collects and prepares edible plants at their own risk. Be aware of legal restrictions on foraging in a particular area, the presence of pollutants and herbicides, and your own allergies and intolerances. Do not harvest a plant unless you are absolutely certain that you have identified it correctly – and even then, it may be advisable to seek assistance from an experienced forager, as some edible plants look nearly identical to poisonous ones. It is recommended that you consult a qualified herbalist or naturopath when seeking natural healthcare advice. Know that some pharmaceutical drugs can have unintended interactions with plant medicine, so it is essential to consult your healthcare professional if you are taking prescription medication. This book is not a replacement for individualised professional advice on health care and wellbeing, and it is not meant to be used to diagnose or treat.

Opposite Cobbler's pegs aka farmer's friend (*Bidens pilosa*), used as food and medicine.

My foraging journey

Growing up on a dairy farm in northern Italy, foraging was a regular part of my life. As it is on most farms, there was always a job to do. We produced labour-intensive corn, wheat and oats as animal feed, together with hay – which was stored away for the colder months when fresh grass was not available. Our main income was generated by the milk that we supplied to our local dairy co-op. Unlike modern-day, large-scale monocultural farms, we also raised chickens, pigs, goats, geese, ducks, turkeys and rabbits on a small scale. These animals would be butchered on-site, nose to tail – a traditional food-production process that fed our large extended family throughout the year. My mother also kept a small orchard and vegetable patch, which provided fresh produce in the warmer months and helped stock a pantry full of pickles, preserves, and fermented and cured goods to get us through the winter.

'I'm bored' was never an intelligent offering at our place, as new tasks were always in abundant supply: tending to all the animals, milking the cows, cleaning the barn and caring for the calves, as well as ploughing, fertilising, planting, irrigating, pruning and harvesting.

There was also the task of gathering wild plants, the kind of job my mum would usually give me to get me out of her hair. But it was also a way to teach me. My sisters and I would return from the fields with baskets of berries and fruits in summer, wild greens in the spring, and nuts and mushrooms in autumn – after which ensued a process of elimination by Mum. 'Not this one ... not this one,' she would say, tossing the unsuitable offerings aside, followed by a triumphant 'This one!', as she pointed out something edible. And so my education in foraging began: not in a classroom, but out in the fields and woods. Actively familiarising myself with the local ecology – watching, listening, tasting – through a process of trial and error, I gradually acquired my 'plant eyes'. Rather than learning to see 'weeds', I was teaching myself to recognise nutritious, edible sources of sustenance and healing, gifted to us by nature.

While there was never a dull moment, or a holiday for that matter, life was lived simply. Mum was providing three meals a day for our family – Dad, my four sisters and me – while also running the farm and dealing with everything that this responsibility entailed. Her menus were structured around efficiency and availability. I will always remember the oversized pot slowly boiling away on the wood stove, filled with our vegetables and a cut of meat from the freezer. For Mum, prep time was a maximum of ten minutes – then it was a matter of loading the stove with wood, filling the pot and placing it on the hotplate, and returning three hours later to a finished meal. These days it's called slow cooking.

While our 'domesticated' produce was usually cooked this way, the wild food we foraged in the local fields and forest – such as dandelions, nettles, mulberries and mushrooms – were either served fresh or preserved.

* * *

In rural Italy in the 1980s, there was nothing unique or unusual about my family's way of life. Our farm was situated on the dark, wet, rich soil of the floodplains of the upper Po Valley. The fields were small patches of land reclaimed from swamps many hundreds of years before, with medieval irrigation locks, *chiuse*, allowing for regular watering. This is a land laden with a deep respect for produce, cultivation and food. This is Slow Food country.

Our farm sat on the outskirts of a small village, and there were roughly fifty families in the area still working the land in an unbroken continuation of ancient cultivation methods. By the mid-1990s, however, these farming practices were undeniably in decline, due both to the onset of industrial agriculture and to short-sighted EU policies that put restrictions on small farmers to the advantage of bigger agricultural enterprises. We either had to adapt and expand, or disappear.

At the time of writing this book, in this same small village there are only a handful of families still working the land, most of whom have absorbed adjoining fields in order to expand to a profitable size.

In the 1990s, I was in my mid-twenties. I saw the direction in which my country was headed, and I felt discouraged and irrelevant. As is common in the minds of the young and the free, the idea of migrating to a

Previous spread, left Harvesting mushrooms in a pine forest. Here, I am looking for saffron milk caps (*Lactarius deliciosus*) and slippery Jacks (*Suillus luteus*).

new land on the far side of the planet was incredibly attractive and full of possibilities. And so I left.

After arriving on Australia's eastern shores, I spent many years working in orchards and garden centres. I soon learnt that foraging for wild food was generally regarded as an unusual practice, and I saw many of the plants I had been taught to value being wasted. At the same time, I sensed a longing in those around me to rekindle their untapped connection to nature. Loss of Indigenous knowledge and a disproportionate mistrust of wild produce are commonplace in a society where disconnected living is the norm. The names of the so-called weeds growing on our doorsteps have largely been forgotten, and some of the most important food and medicinal plants – plants that have developed alongside humans as our coevolutionary species over the course of millions of years – are distrusted and dismissed. A distinctive moment of realisation happened when I was working in an orchard where the farmer regularly poisoned the dandelions at the base of his apple trees, as it was easier to kill with herbicide rather than cut with a slasher. My disbelief at the orchardist's treatment of such an important food source fuelled my need to educate, to stop this mistreatment of the land and its nutritious gifts.

As a young dad raising a family in rural New South Wales, I wanted to teach my two young daughters to experience seasonal wild food treats, just as my mother had taught me, and to ensure that this knowledge was not lost. Adventures into the forest to seek out and harvest wild mushrooms became activities that extended family and friends soon wanted in on. These were fun, empowering experiences for kids and adults alike, and were to become the basis of the foraging tours I run today.

At this time, I also embarked on a series of short art courses, spurred by a deep-seated passion for the arts and self-expression. This led to a bachelor's degree, which allowed me to connect my foraging skills and love for nature with public art engagements. It gave me a platform to highlight the misuse and waste of weeds by land managers. The knowledge I had brought with me from my birthplace began to emerge through my art practice, as I sought to return botanical literacy to communities through storytelling, exhibitions, commissions and events.

Telling the story of wild plants is my passion. I run public and private foraging workshops week in, week out, and in the process connect personally with over 2000 people every year. My goal is to enable conversations around belonging, sustainability and agency, while eating nutritious and tasty food.

Read this book and find out how you CAN engage with wild food sources, how you CAN reconnect with the old stories of our ancestors, and how you CAN find a sustainable way to interact with and learn from your surroundings, caring for ecologies while transforming your neighbourhood into an edible adventure.

Introduction

The resurgence

Foraging – or at least the *idea* of harvesting wild food from the land – is now out there in the mainstream.

Today, we are confronting interconnected challenges – climate change, food security, pandemic, just for a start – that affect all of us on a worldwide scale, impacting our everyday lives and informing our decision-making processes. In the face of these challenges, we want to empower ourselves with the knowledge and skills that bring self-reliance and equip us to care for our families and communities. We now feel the urgency, and have the opportunity, to create new narratives and move towards coexistence based on shared values of compassion and understanding for all species.

It has been interesting to observe how COVID-19 has prompted a rush to buy seeds and seedlings, an urge to bake and preserve – and a drive to connect with the core people in our lives, creating a solid social nucleus of family and close friends. How, in challenging times, we turn towards a more fulfilling and rewarding existence, built on values, care and love.

Foraging fits well within this sentiment. We humans are, at our core, hunter-gatherers, dwellers of space who lived static lives for hundreds of generations until we became fully accomplished in extracting nutrients and other needs from our surroundings, in a symbiotic relationship with our coevolutionary species.

There is no better example than the Aboriginal and Torres Strait Islander ways of life, anchored in location and framed by narratives of intricate kinships, where land *is* the people, the language, the culture and the point of reference.

The ancient wisdom of Aboriginal cultures, as articulated in their stories, was bypassed and undermined 250 years ago with the process of colonisation, replaced with much younger and less sophisticated systems of exploitation. It is great to witness a resurgence now, with Aboriginal and Torres Strait Islander leaders fronting the need to bring back Indigenous knowledge and practices in the decision-making processes that determine how we use land and resources.

Domestication – subjugation – of vegetation and animals allowed modern society to expand and grow in numbers, but it came at a cost for biodiversity and, ultimately, us. It began relatively recently and simultaneously in various parts of the world about 10,000 to 12,000 years ago. As American anthropologist and historian Jared Diamond states (in an article entitled 'The Worst Mistake in the History of the Human Race'): 'recent discoveries suggest that the adoption of agriculture, supposedly our most decisive step toward a better life, was in many ways a catastrophe from which we have never recovered. With agriculture came the gross social and sexual inequality, the disease and despotism, that curse our existence.'

Agriculture may have existed for more than 10,000 years, but we have only fully adopted a reliance on cultivated produce in the past 100 years, with the advent of industrial agriculture and subsequent monopolisation of distribution.

Three generations ago it was still common practice all over the world to collect wild food as part of our regular intake of nutrients; knowledge of what, where and when to forage was a necessary part of daily life. At the very least, we had some lived experience of harvesting wild food with our own hands.

Two generations ago, wild food harvesting started to decline, coinciding with the advent of supermarket culture, monocultural systems of food production and escalating urbanisation.

One generation ago, the knowledge associated with foraging had mostly been lost. It was no longer put into practice – and that meant that it went to sleep, remaining virtually forgotten. Some of you might have memories of your nanna stopping the car by the side of the road to pick wild fennel, or of feeling mortified as your grandpa collected dandelions in the park for a dinner treat while you nervously looked out for someone from school, afraid they might recognise you harvesting weeds. There was a common sense of shame associated with collecting our food in this way. A sign of low social status, a part of our ethnicity that stopped us from fully behaving as 'normal' Australians.

Today, we want the knowledge back. Pickling and gardening workshops are widespread. Trending social media posts highlight the satisfaction to be found in growing and processing our own food. The popularisation of TV cooking shows testifies to the urgency that modern humans feel in wanting more control over what we eat, how it is grown and where it comes from. Many of us now define ourselves according to what foods we consume and how good and natural those ingredients are, and this is reflected in our language: *organic, local, farm to table, nose to tail, slow-cooked, bespoke, homemade, crafted* – adjectives that are now synonymous with this aspirational lifestyle. And *wild, foraged, native* and *seasonal* foods are extensions of this resurgence.

Foraging for food is the old made new again, but this time it's cool.

So, there's the hook, the marketing ploy. If that's what it takes to get you interested, then it's okay with me. But you should be aware that when you immerse yourself in learning about harvesting wild foods – when you truly *experience* foraging – you activate a number of processes that are empowering and irreversible.

Previous spread, left Buck's-horn plantain (*Plantago coronopus*), a common wild edible of coastal Australia.

Below Assessing a native Port Jackson fig (*Ficus rubiginosa*) for fruits. I spend a lot of time checking in with my local resources to ensure I am ready when the produce is at its best.

A coevolutionary journey

By participating in natural systems as foragers, by enacting our evolutionary role as 'cohabitants', we personally engage with ancestral ways of relating with the environment. Those processes are innate, embedded in our psyche and in our cultural knowledge. We understand ecologies through the eyes of a forager. That entry point can facilitate how we relate to place. When you know your neighbourhood by what it can provide, it transforms from a place that you travel through to a place that you keenly keep an eye on.

Foraging allows us to see value in the landscape. It creates a connection point between us and the ecology around us. We become stakeholders in this new-found wealth, which in turn fosters a sense of genuine care.

The plants that grow uninvited in our immediate surroundings represent the current status of coevolution. They are the result of millions of years of plants and humans exploiting one another. Dandelions, plantain, flatweed, purslane and fat hen are just some of the plants accustomed to humans – and to the things that humans do to nature. Not only have they adapted to the conditions we've created in our settlements, they have evolved to exploit them.

In the same way, humans have also evolved, having extracted nutrients from the wild plants living around us since the earliest days of our history. We then chose to cultivate many of these plants, and through selective breeding and hybridisation these species have become the modern agricultural crops we know today.

It is important to note that even when we, in our part of the world, deem a certain plant a 'weed', without value, it may well be one of the 'chosen' crop foods in another culture. There is a clear bias in our attitude to food plants, driven by tastes and habits that stem from our particular cultural construct. I myself always enjoy the bitter flavours of salad greens like the dandelion, which was a 'usual' ingredient in my Italian upbringing. I would suggest you try a new food plant a little at a time. You'll be surprised how quickly your palate begins to gain an appreciation of these flavours.

Here in Australia we live in a novel ecology, alongside which our native plants and animals coexist with various degrees of ease. The biodiversity of this continent before European settlement is now dispersed among various other species, including all of our agricultural crops, farming animals and of course, us humans. The new species are now part of the narratives of this land, and indeed many have become so ingrained in the ecologies of Australia that they are considered naturalised, to the extent of cross-breeding with native strains.

The stories and cultural practices related to such species are by now intermixed with native narratives too, creating new, localised and deeply 'Australian' stories, such as those around lamb, brumbies, grapes, canola and a host of less-celebrated species like wild dogs, blackberries and exotic field mushrooms.

Celebrating old knowledge

This book wants to inspire. It proposes an approach and lays out an argument. In doing so, it takes you on a journey of discovery, tapping into ancestral relationships with ecologies to rediscover a connected life between us 'urban animals' and the other species living around us. Along the way, it answers the common questions that people always ask me about wild plants. What is it? Can I eat it? How do I make sure I'm not poisoning myself?

Put simply, this book is for anyone who wants to know more about our ecology and our role in it. It is as valuable for kids as it is for expert foragers. Within these pages, parents will find the tools to introduce botanical appreciation into their own and their offspring's lived experiences. Gardeners will find new ways to appreciate their surroundings and learn how to utilise the environmental services that weeds bring to soil, while bush regenerators will find the lines separating good and bad plants blurred. Chefs will uncover new produce, new flavours and new textures, while bushwalkers and nature lovers will discover the names and identifying features of the weeds they walk past every day.

It is also important to know that I have written *Eat Weeds* for and on behalf of those Australians who suffered denigration and ridicule when gathering wild fennel by the roadside or while picking dandelions in the park. When we offer up respect for the old migrant knowledge, the keepers of that wisdom will in turn find validation for their actions – actions that embody the oldest traditions of communion with land.

This book is for anyone who cares to look and wants to learn.

Bulrush (*Typha* species), an ancient food source.

How to use this book

Eat Weeds is divided into ecosystems: backyard, urban streets and parklands, sea, river, and forest. Rather than representing the usual bioregions as defined by scientists, each of these zones is a hybrid, existing between people's understanding of places and the reality of ecologies as altered by human intervention.

I deliberately approached the subject by zones – as opposed to seasons or alphabetical order of plants – so that wherever you are, you will have a clear image of what you can find and how to interact with it. Many plants will be present across several zones, but others will be specific to one particular ecosystem. The index at the end of the book will help you navigate this.

Enter each zone with open eyes, heart and mind. Arguably the best thing you can do to learn about a place is to go there, sit down, shut up and observe. My hope is that this book will give you the eyes to see what has always been in front of you.

Take a step outside. I guarantee that within 3 metres of your doorstep you will find food and medicine growing, awaiting the recognition they (and you) deserve.

WHAT THIS BOOK IS NOT

- This book is not a recipe book, yet it gives plenty of instructions on how to use plants and fungi as food and medicine.

- This book is not a catalogue of flora and fungi in Australia. It is a curated selection of the most common, easily identifiable plants and mushrooms growing in subtropical and temperate Australia, where the majority of us live.

- This book is not a survivalist's guide; rather, it is a celebration of old knowledge. This book comes from a place of abundance, not scarcity.

- This book is not the only book you need. However, it is surely an important addition to your library. I encourage you to buy more books and do more research. It is my hope that *Eat Weeds* will start you on the journey and that you will never stop learning.

- This book is not about native Australian flora. It is about what I term 'botanical reality'. This book is about the plants and mushrooms that manage to exploit and thrive in the great mess that we have made of the land on which we live. Some are native, most are not. This book is about the anthropogenic – the human-made biosphere that we inhabit.

- There are no rare plants on these pages. No endangered species in here. Just plain, omnipresent weeds and the native Australian species that defy our callous inability to share environments.

Toxicities

Harvesting plants from the wild – or, equally, your local park – has to happen with full acknowledgement that there are risks.

The most probable risk is mistaken identification. Follow the clues laid out in each chapter to positively identify a plant. Some plants are obvious, some are not. Learn about one plant at a time. Take it slowly, use common sense.

Even when you know you have identified a plant correctly, please only ever try eating a small amount at first: you might not like the taste or you might find it hard to digest. Just because a plant is edible does not guarantee that you will love it. As a general rule, there is nothing in the world that you should eat by the bucketful. Some species are toxic in large quantities, and that includes some of our everyday fruit and vegetables; if you've ever eaten a kilo of cherries or prunes, you will know what I'm talking about. Just as you would eat a variety of foods in small amounts for a healthy balanced diet, the same goes for eating wild foods.

We also need to consider pollution, particularly if you live in urban and suburban environments. Please be mindful of where you forage. Do some research about the area where you pick your greens before you fill your salads and pies with them. Chances are, the land and water bodies you harvest from have a history of misuse. Be aware that rivers and creeks – many of which have been channelled into concrete-lined flood overflows – are gathering up the waste products of our polluting industries and lifestyles as they flow through our cities and suburbs.

It is possible that the area you want to harvest from has been sprayed with herbicides. Do not harvest from locations where the grass looks dead. Spraying is quite common along footpaths, roads and railways. The easy way to assess the situation is to call your local council, which is legally obliged to let people know where and when it uses chemical herbicides in parks and reserves. You can also obtain a lot of important information from your local bush regeneration group. Importantly, please always thoroughly wash any plant or fruit that you harvest before ingesting it, as you would with any produce you buy at the market.

Do not get disheartened. There are plenty of suitable places to harvest from, right in the middle of the city where you live. Scout your neighbourhood; learn your streets and parks; create a map.

And when you have your 'plant eyes' ready, what's next?

I always finish my workshops by offering four key foraging 'tools'. These tools are simple, empowering notions that will help start you on your journey into the rewarding world of foraging. Here they are, in no specific order of importance.

Positively identify everything

I can't stress enough just how vital positive identification is when you're foraging for wild food. If you intend to eat it and don't want to risk making yourself or others sick, you need to be 100 per cent positive about your identification. There will be lots of plants that have a similar look and behaviour, so please make sure you are fully confident in your ID. Mostly, a wrongful identification will result in a yucky taste in your mouth or a mild stomach upset; however, in some rare cases it can be a life-threatening experience. Do not let this idea discourage you, though. To put things into perspective, I find cycling in Sydney traffic to be a far riskier activity than foraging for wild food.

But please *do* be aware, be responsible and know your limits.

Use books, apps and forums. Go to workshops to learn from experts, or gather knowledge from neighbours who have lived in your area for a long time. Always make sure you know exactly what you are engaging with before you forage.

Take the example of the mulberry. This tree is an incredible teacher. For those of us who had the experience of picking mulberries straight from a tree when we were kids, the shape, feel, look and taste of the berries have been cemented within our lived knowledge. There is no way you will make a mistake in identification if you walk past a fruiting mulberry, because that knowledge is part of you. If someone comes along and asks you whether the berries are cherries or blueberries, you would not second-guess yourself, you would not be confused. You would reply straight away with the correct answer: *'No mate, this is a mulberry.'* That's where you want to be. You want to know at 'mulberry level' anything you plan to eat from the wild. Take your time, accumulate knowledge slowly – one species at a time – and enjoy the process.

If it looks like a stick, it probably tastes like a stick

I know, it sounds a bit silly and obvious, but that's exactly why this foraging tool is so effective. What I mean by this is: trust your eyes. Without even knowing it, you already have much of the knowledge you require; you just need to put it to good use. As an example, think about the choices you make when you are buying herbs. There you are, looking for, let's say, parsley. You spot the bunch of parsley on the shelf, but it looks a bit lifeless, a bit droopy. Perhaps it's a little dry at the edges, and discoloured, or maybe it's even starting to rot at the base. What do you do? Do you buy it and hope it will taste better than it looks? Or do you leave it and either search for a fresher looking bunch or consider a parsley-free recipe instead?

You leave it. Of course you do.

The ability to identify edible produce is already ingrained – it is there in your eyes, in your unconscious assessment of freshness and food potential. If the parsley looks green, juicy, bright, crunchy and fresh, it will probably taste green, juicy, bright, crunchy and fresh. If the parsley looks old, droopy and half-rotten, chances are it will taste old, droopy and half-rotten. The same goes for wild, foraged produce. You have these skills already. Use them.

The best place to forage is your own garden

This is important even if you do not have a garden. What it means is: forage where you know. Forage where you walk every day; where you know who sprays what and how many dogs there are about the place. Forage in areas where you have a confident knowledge of the history of the soil in which those greens are growing. I understand that nowadays many of us live a life on the move, relocating every few years to a new house, suburb, city or state. That's when it becomes important to seek out local knowledge.

Start by learning the name given by the First Nations people to the place where you live; learn who your local Elders are, pay respect.

Go talk with the owner of the local corner store, or a neighbour, or your local environmental action group, where often enough you will get the lowdown on your area, its history and possibilities. Stay put for a while and slowly map your locale. It will be worth it, and in the process you will find belonging and care.

Foraged food is not free food. It's a gift

Please pay respect to resources, particularly native vegetation, as many species are struggling to cope with land degradation and climate change. We need to look after our surroundings. Be kind to nature so that you can come back to it, others can enjoy it, wildlife can use it and the plants themselves can survive and even thrive.

Do not mistreat a plant, even if it is a weed; we have no right to impose on them any more than we already do. Be aware that a plant colony is more than just plants – it is also insects, fungi, bacteria and all the microbiology of the soil intertwined. All of which will be affected by how you treat the plants. Treat each plant colony with care. Use your willingness to take advantage of your local resources as an avenue to build value right in front of your eyes.

There are too many humans on this planet, and it would be next to impossible to replace the fruit and vegetables you buy from the greengrocer with foraged ingredients. The best you can do is to introduce an occasional seasonal treat into your nutritional routine. And that in itself is an incredible gift for your body.

Above all, please only ever harvest where there is abundance, only ever in small amounts, and wherever possible with a clear understanding of the implications of your actions.

In short,
　　　　eat weeds.

Opposite Edible weeds used as food and medicine: shepherd's purse (*Capsella bursa-pastoris*), dock (*Rumex crispus*) and cleavers (*Galium aparine*).

Chapter 01

✳   This chapter will help you find your 'plant eyes' and enable you to recognise food growing where you once only saw weeds.

Backyard

Backyard

Your backyard is the best place to forage.

There is food and medicine growing right outside your door, right now. It has always been there. Our backyard is the most intimate threshold between us and other species, the ones that have learnt to live close to us. It is a place where we experience countless interactions with nature - incidental exchanges, as well as the incredible unfolding of adaptation. There are insects in our backyards, lizards, birds and weeds. Some seem not-so-friendly, but most have a lot to teach us about ourselves and how our actions affect the land around us.

Our backyard is our sanctuary. This little corner of the world, one that we tend to define with a fence and boundary pegs, is both the modern development of the process of domestication that allowed us humans to thrive as a species and the first step into the unpredictable results of our constant reckoning with natural processes.

Our backyard is a place where we define what belongs and wage war against the plants that do not fit into our social construct of what a garden should be. It is here that we see - day in, day out - the delicate dance between invitation and permission. We want to invite nature in, but not too much of it. We want diversity, but only of species we like or consider useful. We want growth and abundance, but keep hacking away at lawns and bushes that exceed the allocated space. We punish nature for its spontaneity and resilience, for doing what *it* wants, rather than what *we* want it to do.

Our backyard is where we learn about weeds.

Many of the 'wild' plants growing in your yard are now termed 'weeds'. They are regarded as pesky, uninvited, stubborn self-starters, yet a great number of them are among the world's most ancient food plants, often offering outstanding medicinal properties. When you take the time to get to know them, you will discover your backyard in fact holds a treasure trove of valuable plants.

You, as guardian of this green space, will know best whether or not pollutants are present. You will get to know the life cycles of the various species. You can pick and choose harvest times and quantities and, ultimately, finetune a sustainable interaction with this precious resource.

By getting to know what grows in your yard you will discover a wilder nature, come to terms with coexistence and hopefully facilitate space for a flourishing biodiversity both in your garden and on your dinner table.

In the following pages, I offer up some of the most common backyard weeds.

Backyard legalities and ethics

Not everyone owns their place, and often enough renters need to seek permission to grow food and alter the garden in any way; indeed, sometimes we are obliged to suppress weeds, even if they are actual food. This needs to be taken into account when opening up to the possibilities of a 'wild garden'. Another important aspect that needs to be considered is the specific toxicities of our frontyards and backyards, which sometimes have high concentrations of lead, mercury or even arsenic, particularly if the property is an old house. It is possible to have your soil tested so that you know you are harvesting from clean ground, the same as you would do if you wanted to grow a vegetable garden.

'Back in the late 80s I studied to be a herbalist, and I learnt that the weeds that grow in our own backyard can be eaten and used for medicinal purposes. I have been collecting these valuable weeds ever since, as I understand that where they grow naturally is where the best nutrients for them to flourish are found. If you've ever tried to grow a dandelion or plantain in your garden, and it soon spreads its seeds and grows elsewhere, then you know you'll be getting the best nutrients from the places where this plant grows. Always watch and listen to nature – she will teach you so much.'

— Pat Collins, herbalist and naturopath, author of *The Wondrous World of Weeds*

Taraxacum officinale

Dandelion

EDIBLE PARTS

leaf, stalk, flower, root

SNAPSHOT

Dandelion is a low-growing herb, with long, toothed leaves radiating from a central crown at the base. It is an annual or biennial, growing to suit conditions, up to half a metre tall and wide, and is naturalised in Australia.

Look-alikes: Lots of plants with a yellow flower and a clock of seeds are confused with dandelions, including sow thistle (p. 43) and flatweed (p. 40). Both of these 'false dandelions' will have several flowers per stalk, while a dandelion will only ever have one flower per stalk. This is a great way of differentiating them at a glance.

Dandelion is the quintessential edible weed, but it is probably best known in popular culture for its promise of wishes granted when you blow the 'parachute' seeds away from the fluffy seed head (sometimes known as a dandelion clock). We also use its flowers and stems to thread daisy chains.

For hundreds of thousands of years, as we have travelled together on our evolutionary journey, humankind has been an accomplice in the spread of this plant – and in return the dandelion has provided us with food and healing. Yet we call it a weed. We demonise it, pull it up whenever we see it, slash it with the mower as soon as it flowers, and generally discourage it from growing in our lawns.

This plant knows us so well; it is used to the way we treat land and ecology, and has adapted accordingly. It is one of the most successful colonisers of disturbed land, sprouting up whenever it finds an opportunity.

I myself see dandelions as the embodiment of nature's wish to gift us with health and food, regardless of how destructive or disrespectful we've been. Dandelions were one of the very first wild plants I came to know. As a young boy, I was sent out into the fields with my sisters to collect its spring blooms, which were considered a seasonal treat by my family. By harvesting the dandelions, I was playing my part in the deep historical relationship that we, as humans, have with wild plants.

Dandelions are an outstanding, beneficial and delicious coevolutionary species. You are almost certain to find them growing within a couple of metres of your back door.

IDENTIFICATION

Leaves and stalks (Fig. 1, ii)

The serrated leaves grow wide and flat in mown lawns – and upright in high grass, when the plant is competing for sunlight. The leaves are dark green, with a light-coloured and hollow midrib. Sometimes the midrib has a red tinge, due to environmental stress (cold or dry weather) or age. The edges of the leaves are deeply toothed, giving the plant its name: 'dandelion' is derived from the French *dent de lion* – lion's tooth. Several tall, hollow, flowering stems arise from the plant's base.

Flowers and seeds (Fig. 1, i)

The flower heads are made up of dozens of yellow, overlapping petals (each one being a flower itself). Each flower head unfurls facing the sun and remains open for one or two days, before it closes to form the seed head. A ball of fluffy mini-parachutes then appears at the top of the stem, ready to be dispersed by the wind.

Fig. 1 *Taraxacum officinale*

Fig. 2 Dandelions (*Taraxacum officinale*) come in a great range of sizes, from a few centimetres to 30–40 centimetres tall.

Root (Fig. 1, iii)

Dandelion has a long taproot, which can grow up to 30 centimetres in length and 4–5 centimetres across.

AS FOOD

You can eat the whole plant: flowers, leaves, stem and root. Dandelion can be rather bitter – particularly the older plant – so it is advisable to eat it in conjunction with other less intensely flavoured greens.

I eat the leaves raw or cooked. When I was a kid, we used to collect the young leaves of early spring, mix them with other greens, add boiled eggs, and season with a simple olive oil, salt and vinegar dressing. My siblings and I got used to the bitter taste; we even came to love it.

Dandelion root can be cooked like parsnip in soups, baked like a potato, or slowly roasted and then ground for a healthy, coffee-like drink.

The flowers can be eaten fresh, cooked in fritters and frittatas, or fermented into a wine. The flower buds can be pickled for an excellent treat, similar to capers. I myself graze on dandelion flowers all the time, straight from the fields; just one or two, picked as I walk by. It reminds me of my youth, which must certainly have some beneficial effect, as it brightens up my day straight away!

AS MEDICINE

In herbal medicine, dandelion is regarded as the king of detox because of its properties as a mild diuretic and laxative. Dandelion infusions are regularly prescribed in cleansing programs and are extremely beneficial as liver and kidney tonics. Dandelion is respected as a good source of antioxidants. It also reduces cholesterol, regulates blood sugar, reduces inflammation, lowers blood pressure, assists in weight loss, reduces the risk of cancer, boosts the immune system, aids digestion and keeps your skin healthy.

In simple terms, dandelion is a superior medicinal plant. Any book that discusses herbal medicine would have a page or four dedicated to it. It is that amazing, and it grows just outside your door.

Dandelion and macadamia pesto

This pesto can be served as a dipping sauce, pasta sauce or condiment. For a thinner pesto, simply add more olive oil.

INGREDIENTS

½ cup macadamias

1½ cups fresh weeds including dandelion, wood sorrel and sow thistle (*weeds are interchangeable with other foraged greens, depending on season – let your tastebuds guide you*)

1½ cups fresh basil (*as your palate gets used to the bitter flavour of many of the weeds available, you can increase the amount of weeds and lessen the amount of basil*)

2 small garlic cloves, crushed

¾ cup shredded parmesan (*leave out the parmesan for a vegan pesto or reduce the amount if you prefer a less cheesy flavour*)

5 tbsp olive oil

Salt and pepper to taste

1. Place the nuts, weeds, basil, garlic and parmesan in the bowl of a food processor and blend until finely chopped.

2. With the motor running, gradually add the oil in a thin, steady stream until well combined.

3. Season with salt and pepper and serve.

Flatweed and cat's ear

EDIBLE PARTS

leaf, flower, root

SNAPSHOT

Flatweed and cat's ear range in height and size according to conditions, from 10 centimetres to half a metre wide. They flower all year round, and are naturalised in Australia.

All hail flatweed, the wonderful edible weed. This plant is easy to identify and grows from Mackay in Queensland all the way across to Carnarvon in Western Australia – in abundance. Its look-alikes are also edible, making this an easy food plant for the novice forager. I know a few elderly Greek people who have frontyards filled with flatweed, on purpose, because they love it so much and use it all the time as a generic green in pies.

I myself eat this plant just as often. Whenever I find an attractive specimen, I bring it home and cook it in sauces, stir-fries, stews and veggie rolls, or serve it raw in salsa verde, a parsley-based green dip that I either eat with bread or use as a marinade.

There is no chance you have a lawn and not flatweed.

Many people dismiss it, as its hairiness can be off-putting – and it often gets a bit battered due to its love of high-traffic locations – but when you find a good-looking flatweed, you should definitely try it.

Flatweed (*Hypochaeris radicata*) and cat's ear (*Hypochaeris glabra*) are very similar to the related dandelion, in that all three have a yellow flower made up of dozens of overlapping petals, arising from a flat rosette with a central crown. In Australia we also have another less common variety of flatweed, with white flowers, called *Hypochaeris albiflora*, which is mostly found around Brisbane and Sydney. In the rest of the continent, you will find either *Hypochaeris radicata* or *Hypochaeris glabra*. All edible, all worth your effort to bring to the table.

Fig. 1 *Hypochaeris radicata*

Fig. 2 Flatweed (*Hypochaeris radicata*), spreading out.

IDENTIFICATION

Leaves and stalks (Fig. 1, ii)

The leaves of both flatweed and cat's ear are club-shaped, with rounded indentations – as opposed to the deeply toothed leaf of the dandelion. They are dark green on both sides and can grow up to 30 centimetres long and 5 centimetres wide. Flatweed's leaves are noticeably hairy while those of cat's ear can be less so.

The easiest way to tell the look-alikes apart is to pay attention to the flower stalks. In flatweed and cat's ear they are branched and solid, while dandelion's flower stalks are hollow and never branched, and sow thistle's stalks are branched and hollow.

Flowers and seeds (Fig. 1, i)

The flowers of flatweed and cat's ear are typical of the dandelion family, with cheerful yellow petals that last a few days, closing at night and reopening in the morning – until one day they reappear as a ball of seeds, each with its own white fluffy parachute, ready to be transported by the wind. *Hypochaeris albiflora* has white flowers.

Root (Fig. 1, iii)

Flatweed has a long taproot, at times growing 30 centimetres deep, while the root of cat's ear is shallower and more branched.

AS FOOD

All parts of flatweed plants are edible; however, the leaves and taproot are most often harvested. The leaves range in flavour from slightly bitter to bland. They can be eaten raw in salads, but are most often steamed or tossed in a pan with oil and garlic and served with lemon and salt. It is best to select younger leaves, as they can become fibrous and stringy when older.

The flowers can be collected all year round, with a spike in flowering occurring in the cooler months after rain. They can be infused in honey for a breakfast treat, or coated in flour for colourful fritters. The petals can be used in rice-paper rolls, or as a garnish for salads or cakes.

The root can be dug out, scrubbed, lightly roasted and ground for a satisfying coffee substitute.

I do not know of many wild plants that can be harvested 365 days a year – and that makes this plant one of my most beloved wild veggies.

Sonchus species

Sow thistle

EDIBLE PARTS

leaf, stalk, root

SNAPSHOT

Sow thistle is an excellent adaptor, ranging in height from 30 centimetres in harsh conditions to 2 metres tall when growing in good soil. It basically grows to suit the conditions, usually with a short cycle of a few months, but can survive several seasons if the circumstances allow it. There are three species of sow thistle in Australia: one native, *Sonchus hydrophilus*; and two introduced species, *Sonchus asper* and *Sonchus oleraceus*. All are edible. Sow thistles can be found year round on this side of the world. At any given time, you are bound to find a sprouting, flowering, seeding or dying example of the genus *Sonchus*.

Fig. 1 *Sonchus oleraceus*

Sow thistle (aka milk thistle) is *everywhere*. It grows in a range of ecosystems, from tropical to arid, appearing among farm crops as well as in backyard gardens. All over the world. Sow thistle produces thousands of seeds (as many as 25,000 per plant), and each one of them has a 90 per cent chance of germination. Yes, we are talking about a highly skilled invasive, but that is not necessarily bad – sow thistle is edible, and is a celebrated food plant in lots of cultures.

I am always impressed by just how many advocates this plant has. Whenever I introduce sow thistle to the public, I usually find that someone in the crowd is quite familiar with it and its traditional edible uses. This is often a person with Italian heritage, who offers a simple solution for dealing with this common weed: 'a quick boil, a little oil, lemon and salt and that's it! Enjoy!' Or a New Zealander, who quite proudly declares the plant to be *puha*, a key ingredient in the family tradition of a 'boil up', cooked as part of a pork stew.

One suggested origin for the sow thistle's common name is the British farming tradition of giving the plant to female pigs (sows) to increase their milk production after they have given birth to a litter of piglets.

Despite its unpredictable behaviour and variability in leaf shape, sow thistle is easy to identify through a few distinctive features, including its multi-flowered stalks. You no doubt walk past it every day. As soon as you start to pay attention, you will be able to spot it around your garden, down at the park and at the back of the school. You just need to familiarise yourself with its 'style', and off you go – you will never be able to un-see sow thistle again.

IDENTIFICATION

Leaves and stalks (Fig. 1, ii)

Sow thistle's leaves are deeply toothed, even more than dandelion leaves, and sometimes the edges are tipped with sharp spikes (*Sonchus asper* typically more so than the other two species). The leaves radiate out of the basal crown, but also grow in a smaller form clasping around the flowering stalk.

Although they are similar in many ways, the difference between a flatweed and the sow thistle is the structure of the stalk: the stalk of the sow thistle is hollow and tubular, like a straw; a flatweed's stalk is solid.

All sow thistles have a milky sap, visible when you break the stem. The Māori people of New Zealand used this sticky sap as chewing

gum, and it is known in many cultures worldwide (including Africa, Asia and Europe) for its medicinal properties. Some say that this white sap gives sow thistle its other common name, milk thistle.

Flowers and seeds (Fig. 1, i)

The best identification feature for all sow thistles is the flower. In shape, colour and behaviour it is similar to that of the dandelion and flatweed: bright yellow, opening up when the sun is out and closing at night. And just like the dandelion and flatweed, it has a fluffy seed head, with seed 'parachutes' that are blown away in the wind.

The difference between dandelion and sow thistle is the number of flowers per stalk: sow thistle will always have several flowers per stalk; dandelion will only ever have one flower.

Root (Fig. 1, iii)

Sow thistle's root ranges from a deep single taproot to branched, according to the conditions it finds itself growing in.

AS FOOD

Sow thistle tastes best young. As the plant gets older and starts to flower, it becomes progressively more bitter, making it tastier as a cooked vegetable. The best part of the plant is the young, soft leaves, eaten raw or cooked; they are reminiscent of lettuce or radicchio. I add them to salads, cook them like spinach or use them in soups. You can also eat the young stems, fried in butter or gently steamed and served with oil, lemon and salt.

A friend of mine allows sow thistle to germinate freely in his garden and uses it as a microgreen. He lets it grow for a week or two, and then harvests it for the salad bowl or as a generic green to serve with stews and roasts. I think it is a brilliant idea to take advantage of the high germination rate and exploit the weedy potential of the plant.

AS MEDICINE

The plant is quite high in vitamins and minerals, making it a great tonic. The sap is very effective in removing warts: apply daily, directly onto the wart, which will dry up and crumble away. I remember teaching this remedy to a friend of mine who had just such a problem; each day, when we met up to walk her dog, we would find some sow thistle and apply it to the wart. It took less than two weeks for it to disappear.

Fig. 2 (opposite) Sow thistle (*Sonchus oleraceus*)

Amaranthus species

Amaranth

EDIBLE PARTS

leaf, stalk, flower, seed

SNAPSHOT

Amaranth is an erect branched annual herb that grows from seed. It ranges in form from a low-lying sprawler to a tall bush up to 2 metres high.

Amaranth is an ancient grain, one of the first wild plants to be domesticated – in Central America, over 10,000 years ago. The value of this highly nutritious plant was recognised by the mighty Aztec civilisation, which used amaranth in its religious ceremonies. This esteem is mirrored today by our recognition of amaranth as a super food. There are about seventy species worldwide, all edible. Many of these have now become successful colonisers, making amaranth a reliable source of wild food in a number of cultures. Several of the species turn into tumbleweeds when they die off, helping the spread of the seeds.

The most common weedy amaranths in south-eastern Australia are green amaranth (*Amaranthus viridis*), white amaranth (*Amaranthus albus*) and the native species *Amaranthus mitchellii*, *Amaranthus powellii* and *Amaranthus interruptus*.

IDENTIFICATION

Leaves and stalks (Fig. 1, ii)

The diamond-shaped leaf has a long stalk and varies from the bright emerald of green amaranth to the three colours of tricolour amaranth: green, yellow and red. Sizes vary greatly, from 2–12 centimetres long. The ribbed branches are fibrous and can vary in size and colour.

Flowers and seeds (Fig. 1, i)

Amaranth forms a flowering spike in the intersection between leaf stalk and branch, towards the top of the plant. The flowers are tiny and mimic the plant in colour. The spike is often heavy with seeds, causing it to bend downwards, which gives it a 'nodding' look. The seeds are small, about 1 millimetre in diameter, and either brown or black.

AS FOOD

Amaranth is renowned for its highly nutritious seeds. Although very small, they are easy to harvest. The seeds can be cooked whole, but it is advisable to either crush them first or sauté them in a pan; this breaks down the outer skin encasing the seed and facilitates digestion. Amaranth seeds can be ground in a flour, cooked in porridge or added to salads after 'popping' them. The leaves are harvested green and cooked like spinach, in pies, curries and soups; the stems and flower clusters can be used in the same way.

i

ii

Fig. 1 *Amaranthus viridis*

Amaranth is both cultivated and wild-harvested by many cultures for its leaves and grains; Indigenous Australians have traditionally harvested native species. It is a celebrated food in south India, where it is known as *kuppacheera*, with the leaves being cooked in vegetable dishes. In Greece, where it is known as *vlita*, the leaves are boiled and served with olive oil and lemon.

I have green amaranth growing like a weed in my garden, all through the more traditional veggies. I harvest it whenever I go out to get some green leaves for whatever I am cooking. It is highly versatile, and here in Sydney it produces leaves for about five months, from November to April. The range would be similar elsewhere in south-east Australia.

Fig. 2 Green amaranth (*Amaranthus viridis*) seedlings. This common exotic is found all over Australia, including in deserts and the tropics.

Fig. 3 Green amaranth (*Amaranthus viridis*): a very common
exotic of great nutritional value.

Fig. 4 Red amaranth (*Amaranthus cruentus*), commonly cultivated as a grain source, is now establishing wild populations.

Plantain

leaf, seed

SNAPSHOT

Plantain has layered leaves radiating out from the central crown, and a distinctive tall flowering spike. Plantains are considered perennial plants, and even when cut or stomped upon they will sprout back from the root cluster.

This plant is extremely adaptable; it develops as a low-lying (2–4 centimetres high) herb in the lawn, but grows taller among high grass, with flowering spikes up to 50–60 centimetres in height. It is regarded as one of the plants most likely to be found in the middle of nowhere, left and right of the track, making it a very important plant in survival situations: edible, medicinal, available everywhere.

Fig. 1 *Plantago lanceolata*

Plantain is a widespread weed, found all over the world. In Australia it grows in all states and territories, all the way up to the tropics.

The most common species here is ribwort plantain (*Plantago lanceolata*) – pictured opposite – which grows wherever there's space. Highly adaptable, it can withstand full sun and degraded soils. It survives foot traffic and is most likely to grow where other plants cannot, often sprouting from cracks in the footpath. This peculiarity has influenced a number of its common names; in England, for example, it's sometimes called 'waybread' or 'wayfarer'. Its scientific name, *Plantago*, is derived from the Latin word for 'footprint', which suits it perfectly – partly because it grows in places where it is stomped on, but also because it was customary practice during the Middle Ages for pilgrims to insert plantain leaves in their shoes to soothe their weary feet while travelling.

There are also a number of native Australian plantains, such as *Plantago cunninghamii* or *Plantago debilis*, much respected as both food and medicine in western New South Wales and known as bush bandaid or bush porridge. Aboriginal people traditionally bruise the seeds and mix them with water to create a satisfying and filling meal.

Other plantains of note are broadleaved plantain (*Plantago major*), mostly found in waterlogged environments, and buck's-horn plantain (*Plantago coronopus*), quite common in coastal areas where it can withstand salty conditions (see p. 145).

All of the species discussed here are used as food and medicine.

IDENTIFICATION

Leaves (Fig. 1, ii)

Some plantain species have narrow, lance-like leaves (*Plantago lanceolata*, *Plantago cunninghamii* and *Plantago debilis*), while others have wider leaves (*Plantago major*). *Plantago coronopus* has antler-like, lobed leaves, hence its common name, 'buck's-horn' plantain. All species share the distinguishing feature of three to seven parallel veins running along the full length of each leaf.

Flowers and seeds (Fig. 1, i)

Another typical and very recognisable feature is the flowering spike, which springs up on a tall stalk, somewhat resembling a microphone. The flowers are very small, insignificant, usually white and short-lived. The spike produces small (1–2 millimetres), round seeds after pollination.

AS FOOD

Plantain is not the tastiest plant as food, the leaves being coarse, highly fibrous and somewhat bitter. It is best to select young leaves and blanch them; alternatively, cook the leaves thoroughly before enjoying them as part of a meal.

The tiny seeds are also harvested. They are either ground, to be added to soups or bread, or soaked in water to create a porridge.

AS MEDICINE

I use plantain as an emergency bandaid, as it quickly stems blood flow and encourages the repair of damaged tissue. If I cut or scratch myself, I find plantain, crush the leaf and apply it directly onto the wound.

I make a skin salve with plantain and chickweed (see p. 55), which I use regularly for scratches, irritated skin, abrasions or when I get a thorn stuck under the skin. It quickly heals the wound, settles the irritation and even draws out the thorn! This salve is so simple to make and such an all-rounder that I regularly gift little pots to friends and family, and they all love it.

I also use plantain for the preparation of a cough syrup, sometimes adding horehound (*Marrubium vulgare*) to the syrup for its expectorant properties.

Plantain cough syrup

Makes 500 ml

INGREDIENTS

4 cups young ribwort plantain leaves

1½ cups sugar

HOW TO STERILISE JARS

Wash your glass jars in soapy water and rinse thoroughly. Place the jars on a baking tray in a cold oven and heat to 110 °C. Leave the jars in the 110 °C oven for about 10 minutes or until they are completely dry. It's best to do this just before you are ready to fill them.

Wash and rinse the lids separately, then put them in a saucepan, cover completely with water and bring them to the boil. Boil for a couple of minutes, then drain and dry thoroughly.

1. Collect 4 cups of young ribwort leaves – make sure you pick young and healthy-looking leaves. Wash them and chop into small pieces.

2. Add the plantain to a saucepan with 500 ml of water. Bring to the boil, then lower the heat and simmer for 30 minutes.

3. Allow to cool and then strain the water through a cloth (it is good practice to get yourself a cheesecloth for this step). Discard the leaves.

4. Put the strained plantain water in a saucepan over a low heat and mix in the sugar, stirring until it has dissolved.

5. Fill sterilised jars with the water and sugar mixture while it is still hot. When it cools down, it will be thick, sweet syrup. It will keep for at least a year in the fridge.

Stellaria media

Chickweed

EDIBLE PARTS

leaf

SNAPSHOT

Chickweed is an annual herb, with slender stems that grow along the ground. You will most likely find it in your garden beds and under your trees. I say that chickweed in your garden is a badge of honour, not a curse, as it means that your soil is happy and healthy. The whole plant is bright pea-green.

The easy way to identify this plant is by looking closely at the stems, where you will notice a single line of hairs on one side only, like the crest of a chicken. And then, if you tease the stems apart you will notice an internal core, like a bone: chickweed has a chicken crest and a chicken bone.

Some plants are just great seasonal markers. These annuals will thrive in a specific season, disappearing when the temperature drops or, in the case of chickweed, appearing and invading your garden once the colder months settle in.

Chickweed is a little herbaceous plant that occurs all over south-eastern Australia, with records showing it growing all the way up into the tropics. It is an exotic, although naturalised in Australia. A celebrated edible and an outstanding medicine, chickweed is easy to identify once you know what to look for. So here goes – the hunt for chickweed begins.

IDENTIFICATION

Leaves and stalks (Fig. 1, ii)

Chickweed leaves, which occur opposite one another, are oval in shape, tapering to a pointy end. They grow 1–3 centimetres long and 5–15 millimetres wide. The stems are round in cross-section and have a single line of hairs running along their length.

Flowers and seeds (Fig. 1, i)

The flowers are tiny and white, and have five peculiar petals shaped like a 'V' (making it look like there are ten of them). The fruit is an oval capsule with red-brown seeds inside.

AS FOOD

Chickweed is mostly eaten raw. The whole plant is edible, but the stalks tend to be fibrous. Chickweed is most commonly used as a green in sandwiches and salads, or as a side dish and/or garnish, and can be added to smoothies together with other greens or fruits. Please be mindful that as the plant gets older, it gets more and more stringy.

Fig. 1 *Stellaria media*

Fig. 2 Chickweed (*Stellaria media*), food and medicine found in everyone's garden.

AS MEDICINE

Chickweed has a very long history of herbal use, being particularly beneficial in the external treatment of any kind of skin irritation. It has been known to soothe severe itchiness when all other remedies have failed. Chickweed can be applied as a poultice to relieve skin rashes, or you can add an infusion of the fresh or dried herb to bathwater, as its emollient properties will help to reduce inflammation (in rheumatic joints for example) and encourage tissue repair. I most often prepare a skin salve with it, infusing the chickweed in oil, together with some plantain. This simple home remedy is great for healing scratches and little scars, and for use generally in soothing irritated skin.

Makes 3 cups

Chickweed and plantain skin salve

INGREDIENTS

½ cup fresh chickweed leaves

½ cup fresh plantain leaves

1½ cups olive oil

½ cup beeswax

1 cup shea butter

1. Lay the chickweed and plantain on a tray and leave for a couple of days, away from direct sunlight, to dry out completely.

2. Finely chop the dried chickweed and plantain and place in a sterilised jar (see p. 52). Cover completely with the olive oil. Stir to make sure there are no air bubbles.

3. Leave to infuse in a cool, dry place away from direct sunlight for 2–4 weeks.

4. Strain the oil through some cheesecloth into a bowl, squeezing out all of the herbal juices.

5. Using a sharp knife, cut the beeswax into small pieces. The smaller they are, the more easily they will melt. Set aside.

6. Place a small heatproof bowl in a shallow saucepan filled with water or use a double boiler if you have one. Gently simmer the water over a low heat. Do not bring to the boil.

7. Once your water is simmering, transfer the infused oil to the heatproof bowl. Mix the shea butter with the oil and let it melt, stirring with a spoon to help the process, then add the beeswax and stir until the mixture is smooth and fully combined. Make sure that no water gets into the mixture.

8. While the mixture is still warm, transfer it to sterilised jars. It's now ready to use! Store in a cool, dry place away from direct sunlight. This salve will keep for up to a year.

Portulaca oleracea

Purslane

EDIBLE PARTS

leaf, stalk, flower, seed

SNAPSHOT

Purslane is a succulent herb that grows flat along the ground. It is an annual, appearing each year as Australia's weather warms up in October/November and developing into big, ground-covering mats by the end of summer. The plant spreads from a central crown and can grow up to 50 centimetres wide.

Purslane is a summer plant, spreading its crawling branches out over the scorched ground of Australia in the warmer months – just as it does worldwide. The plant is 'cosmopolitan', meaning it is native to most of the world, including Australia.

Despite records showing use of purslane as food and medicine for thousands of years, these days its beneficial qualities are mostly disregarded. People think of it more as a coloniser of disturbed, depleted soil – as a problematic weed.

There are about twenty species of purslane in Australia, most of which are only found inland in desert conditions or north in the tropics, where they are used extensively by Aboriginal and Torres Strait Islander peoples.

In south-eastern Australia, the purslane in your garden would most probably be common purslane, *Portulaca oleracea*. Lucky me (being a Sydneysider), as it is a magnificent, highly adapted and highly nutritional plant.

IDENTIFICATION

Leaves and stalks (Fig. 1, i)

The leaves are fleshy, rounded and flat, 1.5–2.5 centimetres long and up to 1 centimetre wide. Purslane's stalks are green, but can become red-purplish when older or stressed by lack of water. They can extend and branch out up to 50 centimetres along the ground.

Flowers and seeds

Purslane's yellow flowers are 3–6 millimetres wide, with five petals, and only appear in the middle of the day for a few hours. The fruit is a small lidded capsule, 3–4 millimetres wide, filled with tiny black, shiny seeds.

AS FOOD

This plant is extremely nutritious, famously providing high levels of protein and omega-3 fatty acids, as well as a host of minerals and vitamins. Definitely a weed you want to eat.

I eat purslane all through summer, in cooked dishes or raw in salads. The whole plant is edible: flowers, leaves, stalks and seeds. Young leaves and fresh stalks are best when eaten raw. The flavour is sour and sometimes salty, and the leaves and stems have a juicy texture. Older stalks can be cooked in pies and stir-fries, holding their shape and retaining a crunchy consistency.

In Australia, desert purslane grows in rather large mats. Traditionally, it is harvested and set aside in big piles; the seeds will drop from the plants in a matter of days and can be collected easily, before being mixed with water or an egg to make seed cakes.

i

Fig. 1 *Portulaca oleracea*

Purslane is also eaten throughout much of Europe, the Middle East, Asia and Central America, and among migrant communities in Australia. Traditional recipes from Mexico – where it is known as *verdolaga* – see it cooked in a pork stew or fried with eggs. In Greece – where it is known as *andrakla* – purslane is served raw in salads with feta cheese, garlic, tomatoes and olive oil. In Portugal it is called *beldroegas* and is an ingredient in soups.

Oxalis species

Wood sorrel

EDIBLE PARTS

leaf, stalk, flower

SNAPSHOT

Wood sorrel is an annual or a perennial plant, depending on the species, growing up to 30 centimetres tall and forming clusters 2–3 metres in width. This plant can be in flower for most of the year, and it is important to wait for the flowering to confirm identification, as it can easily be confused with clover.

Lemony in flavour, with beautiful heart-shaped leaves and showy yellow or sometimes purple flowers, wood sorrel is easy to find and to love. It is one of the most plated garnishes in high-end restaurants, its leaves and flowers being used as dish-toppers as well as decoration for craft cocktails.

Wood sorrel is common and widespread, usually found lurking under other plants, where it is shaded and protected. Certain types of wood sorrel produce little onion-like bulbils at the base, while others have branched roots. There are several species of 'weedy' wood sorrels in Australia, including a few natives; those most likely to be found growing in gardens in south-eastern Australia are the exotic species *Oxalis pes-caprae* and *Oxalis corniculata* (pictured opposite).

Wood sorrel is often seen growing in with potted plants. My mum, an avid gardener, always lets it be when it appears, as wood sorrel helps to retain moisture in the soil, with the little 'onions' acting as an emergency reservoir of moisture for the other plants living in the container.

Please note that wood sorrel contains oxalic acid, which gives this plant its sharp flavour. Perfectly safe when eaten in small quantities, wood sorrel should not be eaten in large amounts, as oxalic acid can bind to calcium in our bodies, acting as an anti-nutrient (blocking the absorption of nutrients) or forming kidney stones. The quantity of oxalic acid will be reduced if the plant is boiled and any cooking water discarded, as the water-soluble oxalates are what you want to avoid. Oxalic acid – which is present in many of our commonly eaten vegetables – should be avoided by people suffering from rheumatism, arthritis, gout, kidney stones or hyperacidity.

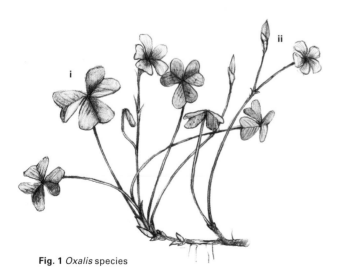

Fig. 1 *Oxalis* species

Leaves and stalks (Fig. 1, i)

The plant's leaves are comprised of three leaflets, superficially similar to those of clovers – but heart-shaped as opposed to oval. Some ornamental wood sorrels have triangular-looking leaves. The stalks can be quite long and are often the juicier part of the plant.

Flowers, fruit and seeds (Fig. 1, ii)

Wood sorrel flowers have five petals, fused at the base to form a cup, and can vary from a few millimetres to 2 centimetres in width. Petal colour varies from white to pink to purple, with yellow being the most common. The fruit is a small capsule containing several seeds.

AS FOOD

You can eat the stalks, flowers and leaves, either raw or cooked – they have a fresh, sour, lemon flavour that makes them a pleasant addition to mixed salads. In South Australia, the plant is known as 'soursob' and is a common snack for children on their way to school. I learnt this soursob story from fellow foragers and now do just the same, regularly snacking on the leaves as I walk. English recipes from the medieval period show that wood sorrel sauces were served with fish and game.

Malva species

Mallow

EDIBLE PARTS

leaf, flower, seed

SNAPSHOT

Mallow is easy to identify by its distinctive five-petalled flower and its 'cheese wheel' seed pod. An annual/biennial plant, it can reach up to 2 metres tall in the case of *Malva sylvestris*, but mostly grows as a cluster of low bushes, 20–40 centimetres high (*Malva neglecta* and *Malva parviflora*).

A Jordanian lady once told me the story of *khubeizah*, a very important plant in Arabic culture – from Jordan to Egypt, Tunisia to Palestine – which has been celebrated since antiquity for its benefits and as a key ingredient in many a dish. The story goes that in the Middle East this common weed is known as the plant of the poor, or 'Arab bread', for even in times of dire need, when food is scarce, people can still find mallow in abundance and so are able to eat.

I now have a garden full of it, because I love it so much. It gives me food for most of the year and needs little to no care. In my book that translates to bonus, bonus and bonus!

Mallow grows all over the world, naturalised on every continent. In Australia, the most common species of mallow are the exotic *Malva sylvestris* (tall mallow); *Malva neglecta* (dwarf mallow); and the impressive *Malva parviflora* (small-flowered mallow), which is found throughout the continent, including arid inland areas and the tropics. Then there is the native hollyhock (*Malva preissiana*), which is widespread in New South Wales, South Australia and Western Australia. You are bound to find mallow in your neighbourhood, if not your own garden.

Mallow is commonly regarded as a weed, but it is neither problematic nor invasive. It grows wherever soil has been disturbed, but does not compromise natural bushland or create problems for the agricultural industry – hence it is not a declared noxious plant in any Australian state. So, put down your herbicide and get to know just how good this plant is.

IDENTIFICATION

Leaves (Fig. 1, i)

The leaves are wide – sometimes as big as 15 centimetres – and palmate in shape, resembling a hand with the fingers spread out. Five to seven veins extend along each leaf, radiating out from where the base of the leaf meets the stalk; this connecting point is darker in colour, and in older leaves appears purple.

Flowers and seeds (Fig. 1, ii)

The flower has five petals and the colour varies from white to pink to purple. The colour is quite important in identification, as there is a very similar plant living in the same environment as mallow that has a RED flower. Not pink, not purple, but RED. The name of the plant (you guessed it) is red-flowered mallow (*Modiola caroliniana*). It is not a true mallow, but if you harvest it by mistake, don't worry. It still is –somewhat – edible. Not great-tasting at all, though, so do check the colour.

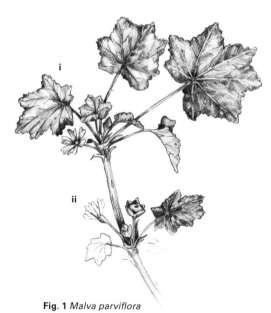

Fig. 1 *Malva parviflora*

Fig. 2 Small-flowered mallow (*Malva parviflora*)

The seed pod of mallow is shaped like a wheel of cheese, and if you break it open you will find little wedges inside: the seeds.

Root

Mallow has a deep, long taproot for seeking out water and nutrients. If it hasn't rained for months, mallow will be among the last plants that remain alive (handy in Australia!).

AS FOOD

Mallow was recorded as an important food source as early as the 3rd century BCE, when Greek physician Diphilus commended it as part of a healthy diet. In the 1st century BCE, Roman poet Horace recorded in his *Odes*: '*Me pascunt olivae, me cichorea levesque malvae.*' 'As for me, olives, endives and mallows provide sustenance.'

But appreciation of the mallow is not only old news: many cultures still use this common plant today, in dishes such as mallow leaf salad from Turkey; or mallow cooked in oil from Palestine; or stuffed mallow leaves from Greece. And there is so much more, like *horta* pie, mallow and bulgur grains, tabouli … No kidding, look into it. The internet is full of ideas for this plant. It is not a weed, it truly is *food*.

In my house we can't go past a simple mallow fry-up, with olive oil and salt. Or my favourite, fried mallow with Moroccan eggs.

AS MEDICINE

In traditional medicine, mallow is used to soothe irritation of the mouth and throat, as well as dry cough and bronchitis, and it is brewed as a tea in the case of stomach and bladder complaints. Mallow leaves are used as a poultice to treat open wounds, and are laid directly on the skin or added to bathwater to alleviate skin irritations.

When I was a young boy, my mum used to take my sisters and me to the local *mansinoira* (herbal remedy lady) whenever we had a sore tummy or were restless or agitated. The herb lady invariably prescribed us mallow tea to calm the upset organs and to settle our restlessness too. True story.

Chenopodium album

Fat hen

EDIBLE PARTS

leaf, seed

SNAPSHOT

Fat hen is a tall annual or biennial plant that grows up to 2 metres high and spreads to 1 metre across. The overall shape of the plant is conical, and it usually features a single, erect, ribbed central stalk with stripes running along its length. *Chenopodium album* is easily recognised by the dusty coating on the underside of the younger leaves, which gives it a silvery look.

Fat hen is an ancient food plant, celebrated across the northern hemisphere, from the United Kingdom to India, Japan and North America. There are countless records of the plant being found in the earliest human settlements, indicating that it was a part of their diet.

There are several related native and exotic *Chenopodium* species in Australia, ten of which are quite widespread. All the species in the genus are edible, but the descriptions that I give here apply to the common exotic, *Chenopodium album*. I love it because it is very nutritious, and because it looks awesome. I have crafted several walking sticks from the main stalk of the plant. They are light, flexible and very strong – excellent companions for my long walks.

Fat hen has been a key cultural species in all the countries where it grows. Although these days it is mostly regarded as a weed of crops, there is a resurgence in the perceived value of this plant and the benefits it brings to our nutritional landscape. I tend to harvest this plant and then dry and store the leaves for future use. I add a bunch of them whenever I'm making a soup or a root vegetable casserole.

Fig. 1 *Chenopodium album*

Please note that fat hen contains high levels of oxalic acid and should only be consumed in moderation or as part of a balanced diet. (See wood sorrel, p. 58, for further information.)

IDENTIFICATION

Leaves and stalks (Fig. 1, ii)

The leaves occur alternately up the stalk, and new sprouts emerge from the fork of the stems. Diamond-shaped, with jagged edges, and up to 12 centimetres long and 10 centimetres wide, the leaves are said to resemble geese feet! The under-surface of the new leaves often features a white, flour-like coating, which can be rubbed off.

The single, hairless, central stalk is multi-branched, and can have red or light-green streaks running vertically along its length.

Flowers, fruit and seeds (Fig. 1, i)

The flowers are green and insignificant, and emerge from the tips of the branches in big clusters. The fruit is a small, green-silver, roundish pod, 1–2 millimetres wide; each pod contains one single seed. These fruits appear in large clusters, making them quite easy to harvest.

AS FOOD

Fat hen is a highly regarded vegetable in many parts of the world, particularly in northern India, where it is cultivated and sold in food markets for use in curries, soups and breads. The flavour is akin to spinach but with a distinctive 'dough-like' taste, similar to that of uncooked bread. Fat hen is very satisfying and filling – even a small quantity of these greens will provide a meal that satiates.

The leaves are the most commonly eaten part of the plant. It is preferable to cook them, as fat hen can hold high amounts of oxalic acid (commonly found in many vegetables). To avoid overaccumulation of these compounds in your digestive system, it is advisable to eat the plant as part of a complex diet.

The seeds are very nutritious, being high in protein (16 per cent), and can be used in soups or sprouted and eaten raw. The seeds should be soaked overnight and then rinsed before eating, to increase the availability of nutrients.

Chapter 02

✳   This chapter focuses on food security, edible cities and the push to manifest a stakeholder mentality by turning parkland into urban farms. It also broaches the need for communities to reclaim botanical literacy.

Urban streets and parklands

Urban streets
and parklands

Imagine a city where food grows everywhere, where street trees are actually a dispersed orchard, where parks and kerb gardens are maintained by locals and planted with an array of vegetables, fruits and nuts.

Imagine a place where we harvest grey water and rain water to irrigate our crops, where we recycle our food waste into precious compost, remaking dirt from our organic waste.

Imagine a neighbourhood where the mulberry tree becomes a community gathering point for two months a year - then it's the fig tree's turn to play host, and so on and so on.

Kids climbing trees to fetch the fruits, grandparents sharing their old recipes to preserve this seasonal abundance, workers grabbing a handful of berries to eat on their lunch break and coming back later for a handful of salad greens to take home for dinner ... this is already possible. Mulberries are all around us, green edibles too. A willingness to take control of our neighbourhood already exists, evident in the many street gardens, guerrilla grafting groups and community composting hubs happening all over our cities right now.

Arguably one of the most sustainable actions we can take today is to turn our cities into edible landscapes, minimising the distance between food production and consumer. Several municipalities around the world are already championing a new understanding of civic interaction with public resources, and it is becoming increasingly common for edible trees to be selected for urban greening.

Let's push, let's make this the new norm. Let's start by recognising the possibility that we *can* generate food in our cities. We *can* overcome pollutants and minimise the use of herbicides in the way we manage our locales. We *can* turn our gardens, parks and streets into social hubs, places of sharing and caring, offering a food source for all. *We are already doing it.*

Streetscape and parkland legalities and ethics

Harvesting from urban environments is riddled with legal restrictions, as everywhere is owned – either by someone or some organisation. In this brief snapshot of the possibilities, I would like to mention a few instances where interaction is tolerated or, indeed, even promoted.

Street trees planted in council strips are usually regarded as fair game as long as you do not damage the plant. Often enough, harvesting mature fruits from side streets or carparks prevents them dropping on the ground and creating mess and/or slippery surfaces. Overhanging trees from private property are also regarded as fair game – legally speaking, if any part of the tree hangs over the boundary of your private property, that part can automatically be cut down by council workers or contractors who need to keep the pathways clear. It is common for urban foragers to collect lemons, oranges, apples, figs, peaches, persimmons and more from the trees of under-harvested gardens. It is good practice to knock on the door of the house before filling your bag. In my experience, most owners are quite happy to share their overabundant harvest in exchange for a jar of jam or pickles. You get fruit and you get to meet your neighbour at the same time.

If you venture further out, to the edges of the city, you will encounter feral fruits in abandoned orchards or along the side roads, as uncultivated colonies establish themselves. Those 'wild' fruits can be an important part of a forager's larder.

Urban gardens, kerb gardens and food forests are a new development in our cities, representing the work of local gardeners who want to transform our urban centres into edible landscapes. The general understanding is that if these gardens are open to the public, it is expected that the public will engage with the produce grown. It is paramount that you only harvest in small amounts, take care of the host plant/tree, and consider giving back to the community by offering help or goods to the people who offer you their trees and fruits.

Opposite Peppercorn tree (*Schinus molle*), a common urban tree with edible fruits.

'There's a feeling that pervades urban wastelands, places where recalcitrant plants and animals carve out niches in rubble and abandonment. I won't say this feeling is as good as the awe you can get in vast wild nature. But it's unto itself. These places are ugly in a way that self-juxtaposes all the beauty you do find. They are uncurated, and even surrounded by the lives of so many millions of people there are things to discover behind broken fences or along almost-inaccessible creek banks. Everything living there resonates with the significance of being an emissary from the future, because if it has learnt to live on human detritus, it and its kin and the emergent ecologies they are creating have very bright prospects.'

— Adam Grubb, co-author (with Annie Raser-Rowland) of *The Weed Forager's Handbook*

Mulberry

Morus species

EDIBLE PARTS

fruit

SNAPSHOT

Mulberry trees are deciduous (they lose their leaves once a year) and grow up to 10 metres in height, forming big, bushy clusters made up of several trees all related to the same root system. They are commonly pruned in all sorts of shapes, but always have long, arching branches that reach to the ground when laden with fruit.

Do you remember pulling on the branches of a mulberry tree in order to reach those deep-purple treats? I distinctly remember my mother scolding my sisters and me every second day for a four- to six-week period during mulberry season because we made such a mess of ourselves! How could we resist? So good, so sweet and so addictive, you just can't stop. There was always one more, even juicier, even sweeter, further up the branches!

There are about 200 species of mulberries. However, of these, only two are found growing wild in Australia: white mulberries (*Morus alba*), from South-East Asia; and black mulberries (*Morus nigra*) – pictured opposite – from the Middle East. Both weedy mulberries can be found in all states and territories, wherever the birds spread their seeds.

The trick to foraging mulberries (as with any other wild fruit tree) is timing. It's best to harvest the fruits in stages, picking the fully ripe ones first, leaving the immature ones for later. Over a period of four to six weeks, you should visit the tree at least three times. By harvesting in stages, you will ensure that you always pick the best, ripest fruits. You will also ease the strain on the branches caused by the weight of the swollen fruit, thus preventing the tree from breaking under the weight of its own produce (yes, it happens). Batch-harvesting also prevents the fruit from spoiling on the tree, so that there's less chance of it becoming infested with fruit flies. And there will be no excess fruit to fall onto parked cars and footpaths, a situation that could infuriate your neighbours – who may then decide to take it upon themselves to cut down the glorious tree (and yes, sadly, this happens too).

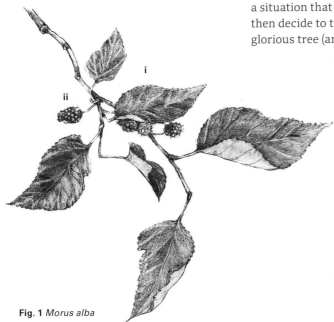

Fig. 1 *Morus alba*

Fig. 2 Squashed black mulberry (*Morus nigra*) – so messy!

IDENTIFICATION

Leaves (Fig. 1, i)

Mulberry leaves are deep green, measuring between 4 and 12 centimetres long. They range from deeply lobed (similar in shape to a hand with fat fingers extended) to heart-shaped, but always have jagged edges. White mulberry leaves are smooth, while the leaves of black mulberries are rough on top and hairy underneath.

Flowers and fruit (Fig. 1, ii)

The flowers appear in springtime, from September to October, forming male and female catkins (elongated, drooping clusters of flowers); sometimes the male and female flowers are found on the same tree. The fruits appear within a few weeks of the flowering, slowly developing from light green to fully purple/black by early summer. Each fruit is made up several small, individual berries, which form a single compound fruit measuring up to 3 centimetres long. The fruits of white mulberries can be white to deep purple, while the fruits of black mulberries are decisively only dark purple, nearly black.

AS FOOD

You can eat the fruits fresh from the tree or cooked in pies, jams, pastes and syrups. They have a delicious and slightly acidic flavour, making them an excellent dessert fruit – which can be eaten in large amounts. The fruit can also be dried and ground into a powder. Pick the ripest berries if you are going to serve them on cakes or with ice-cream; when making jam, however, it is best to pick the slightly unripe fruits, as their acidity will help the jam set. Please remember, before cooking you need to de-stem them. *Every. Single. One.* This may seem a bit fiddly, but it is well worth the effort.

On page 79 is a delicious recipe created by my wife that we prepare during mulberry season to serve with cheese at friends' gatherings.

Fig. 3 (opposite) White mulberry (*Morus alba*), identifiable due to the lack of hairs on the leaves. The fruits of white mulberry can be white to deep purple when fully ripe. Here, you can see ripe and unripe fruits.

Mulberry and rose paste

INGREDIENTS

2 cups mulberries

Oil, for greasing moulds

1 cup caster sugar

Rind of 1 lemon

1 tbsp lemon juice

1 tsp rosewater

1 tsp agar agar powder

We like to make enough paste to serve and to gift, but you can halve or quarter the recipe to suit your own needs.

1. Wash and de-stem the mulberries.

2. You will need moulds for the finished paste. I use small, shallow, dipping-sauce bowls, but smallish flat trays work well too. Prep these by greasing them with oil so the paste will come away easily once set. For this amount of mixture, I use four 10 cm wide by 4 cm deep bowls and fill them three-quarters full; alternatively I use one shallow 20 cm square baking tray.

3. Place the berries in a saucepan along with all the other ingredients.

4. Stir the mixture over low heat until the sugar dissolves. Increase the heat and boil gently for 10 minutes, until the mixture has thickened (the berry liquid needs to boil for at least a couple of minutes to activate the agar agar's setting qualities). Blend with a stick blender.

5. Carefully pour the mulberry mixture into your moulds to a thickness of about 2.5 cm. Cover with a food wrap, such as waxed cloth or foil, then place in the fridge for at least 2–3 hours to set.

6. Once your paste has set, it should resemble a quince paste or thick, firm jelly. Turn the moulds upside down and ease the paste out. It should slide out easily – but if it doesn't, use a knife to coax it out gently. You can keep the paste in an airtight container in the fridge for up to 2 weeks, or better still gift some to your neighbours or friends as a seasonal treat.

7. Serve slices of the paste with a good-quality camembert or as part of a cheese plate with fresh mulberries and nuts.

Syzygium species

Lilly pilly

EDIBLE PARTS

fruit

SNAPSHOT

Lilly pillies are evergreen trees, with a smooth bark. Some species can grow up to 30 metres tall in their natural habitat, while only reaching 8–10 metres in a cultivated or street setting. All species have small oval leaves with a pointed end, and produce a copious amount of flowers prior to their individual fruiting seasons. The best way to identify individual species is when they are in fruit, as the berry of each type of lilly pilly is unique. All fruits contain a single round seed.

In our household, lilly pilly berries are a favourite wild edible – we keep bowls of the fresh, sharp and clove-flavoured treats on hand as a snack when they are in season. Collected by the bucketload, the fruit that we don't devour straight away is pickled – usually with fresh ginger – or turned into jams, pastes, tarts, syrups or sauces. There are several varieties just within a few blocks of our inner western Sydney home, and foraging for these delicious berries has become something we look forward to every year.

There are about sixty to eighty species, found from Victoria all the way to the Northern Territory; most species are native to tropical regions. Four types of lilly pilly in particular – *Syzygium luehmannii*, *Syzygium australe*, *Syzygium paniculatum* and *Syzygium smithii* – are extensively planted in urban settings, often as living screens, by councils and by home gardeners. All lilly pillies produce edible fruit, but the berries of many species are quite sour.

The following four species are widely planted.

Riberry (*Syzygium luehmannii*)

Endemic to northern New South Wales/south-eastern Queensland, this tree (pictured opposite) is extensively planted as a garden hedge. It can take severe pruning, and the continual flush of foliage makes it a preferred tree for use in parks and new housing developments. The flowers are aromatic and white to cream in colour. The pear-shaped berries are light pink to dull red and up to 15 millimetres in length. The fruits have a short season, from around November to December, and present themselves in sizeable clusters of up to a hundred berries.

Scrub cherry (*Syzygium australe*)

The native range of this lilly pilly extends from Batemans Bay in New South Wales all the way along the coast to Mackay in Queensland. The pear-shaped fruit is pink to pale red and up to 25 millimetres long. This tree is extensively planted in private and public gardens for its attractive foliage, pink-red when young and turning a deep green when older. It has been hybridised in a number of dwarf cultivars that are available commercially; their size makes them easy to prune into various shapes. Scrub cherry flowers in summer, with showy displays of white, fluffy flowers. The fruits develop from March to May.

Fig. 1 *Syzygium* species

Magenta lilly pilly (*Syzygium paniculatum*)

This tree is quite similar to the scrub cherry, and the two are often confused. It has a smaller natural range (coastal New South Wales), but is planted in gardens and streets all over Australia. The fruit is pink to pale red, 2 centimetres long, and has a sharp flavour with a crunchy texture, similar to green apples – it is excellent in jams. This lilly pilly flowers in summer, providing plenty of fruit in the autumn months.

Winter or common lilly pilly (*Syzygium smithii*)

This would be the most commonly planted lilly pilly. It is also the one with the most extensive natural range, stretching from Mackay in Queensland all the way to Melbourne. *Syzygium smithii* is easily distinguished by its big clusters of small berries, which vary in colour from white to dull red. The round berries grow up to 15 millimetres in diameter, and often have a depression at the top. There is not much flesh on these fruits, and often the commercial varieties are quite sour. Perhaps not so great to eat fresh from the tree – but in my opinion they make the basis of a tasty fermented beverage. This plant fruits in winter, from May to August, providing fresh berries at a time when they are otherwise scarce.

Fig. 2 Scrub cherry (*Syzygium australe*) leaves and fruit.

Fig. 3 Riberries (*Syzygium luehmannii*): this tree is heavy with fruit for a short season in December.

Lilly pillies and related species are most appreciated for their fruit, which can be used in jams, jellies and pickles (as in the recipe below), and made into syrups and cordials. Australia's early European colonists used lilly pillies as a wild food plant, taking advantage of thousands of years of old knowledge shared by Aboriginal people.

The fruits can be eaten raw, but tend to be sharp, at times bringing a strident acidity. They need to be de-seeded before processing into jams – tedious work, but oh so worth it.

Pickled lilly pilly

Makes four 250 ml jars

These pickled lilly pillies pair well with cheese, salads and roast veggies.

INGREDIENTS

1 kg fresh lilly pilly fruits

1 stick cinnamon bark

4 slices fresh ginger

2 tsp pickling spice

2 cups red wine vinegar

2 cups caster sugar

1. De-seed the lilly pillies by using both your thumbs and forefingers to split the berry in half to reveal the seed. The seed should come away easily. Set the berries aside in a bowl.

2. Sterilise four 250 ml pickling jars (see the sterilising instructions on p. 52). Once the jars have cooled, add a quarter of the cinnamon bark, ginger and pickling spice to each container.

3. Combine the vinegar, sugar and 500 ml of water in a small saucepan over low heat, stirring until the sugar dissolves. Increase the heat, bring the mixture to the boil, then remove the pan from the heat and set aside.

4. Pack the de-seeded lilly pillies into the jars and pour the hot vinegar mixture into each container. Allow the jars to stand for a few minutes. The liquid should reach 1–2 cm from the rim of the jar and fully cover the fruit. You may need to top up the liquid.

5. Seal and label the jars, including the date made. To check that your jars are well sealed, while they are still warm turn them upside down for a few minutes.

6. This pickle keeps for up to a year stored in a cool, dry place away from sunlight. Once opened, it should be kept in the fridge, and will last for up to a month.

Schinus molle

Pink peppercorn or peppercorn tree

EDIBLE PARTS

fruit, seed

SNAPSHOT

The pink peppercorn tree is a handsome evergreen, growing up to 12 metres high, with a wide canopy and weeping form. It develops long branches, and when it is in fruit the red-pink berries make for a beautiful garden feature.

The pink peppercorn is widely planted as an ornamental and street tree in all states and territories of Australia, from Townsville in Queensland, all the way around to Alice Springs in Central Australia and across to Carnarvon in Western Australia. It is drought-tolerant and will flower and fruit for extensive periods. Originally from northern South America, it is now found in warm climates all over the world.

A great way to recognise this tree is by scent, as when you crush the leaves you will instantly notice the very distinctive – in fact, unforgettable – green pepper aroma: sweet, spicy, floral.

IDENTIFICATION

Leaves (Fig. 1, i)

The long, feathery, compound leaves (formed from fifteen to forty-one leaflets) are arranged alternately on the stem, and hang from the drooping branches.

Flowers and fruit (Fig. 1, ii)

Clusters of white flowers develop in springtime, which then produce grape-like bunches of small, red-pink fruits, 5–7 millimetres across, which hang from the tree. The bunches can be up to 30 centimetres long, and when in full colour are quite striking and highly noticeable. These fruits persist on the tree for months, turning cream-yellow as they dry. Each fruit contains a small, spherical, brown-black seed, 3–5 millimetres across: the peppercorn.

AS FOOD

The fruit from the tree is regularly sold as 'pink peppercorn', often replacing traditional pepper (which is not related) in certain dishes. It can be used as a spice in a variety of recipes, both savoury and sweet. As the seeds are quite oily, it is not easy to grind them when fresh, so it is best to dry them fully first. I use the berries sparingly as a spice when I cook (it is rather hot), and love their floral flavour. I add them to roasted potatoes as a spice, and my wife mixes them in with dates, chocolate and almond flour for some very popular energy balls that we offer at big gatherings or festivals.

In Mexico, the fruit is ground, mixed with agave juice and then fermented to make alcoholic beverages. In 2018 I collaborated with Sydney-based Archie Rose Distillery in producing a gin distilled from pink peppercorns, for a special edition featuring wild-harvested botanicals.

Please note that you should treat the berries as pepper, hence only ever ingest small quantities or use as a spice.

Fig. 1 *Schinus molle*

Fig. 2 Peppercorn tree (*Schinus molle*) leaves.

Fig. 3 Peppercorn tree (*Schinus molle*) fruit.

Wild olives: African and European

EDIBLE PARTS

leaf, fruit

SNAPSHOT

Wild olive is a small evergreen tree that grows up to 10 metres tall and 8 metres wide. It can grow in degraded soil, and forms big groves. The tree flowers in spring and produces small, green to dark brown to black berries in late summer. The bark is grey and smooth in young trees, but with age it becomes gnarled and rough, with deep, irregularly shaped grooves.

Most people are unaware that the wild olives 'infesting' south-eastern Australia are edible. These plants are, in fact, prolific producers of nutritious fruits and medicinal leaves. There are three varieties of olives in Australia: two exotic wild olives – European olives (*Olea europaea* subsp. *europaea*) and wild African olives (*Olea europaea* subsp. *cuspidata*) – and one native olive, *Olea paniculata*.

The introduced wild olives were first brought to Australia back in the early 1800s, as both an agricultural crop and a fast-growing, low-maintenance hedging plant. The naturalisation of this introduced tree was accelerated by seed dispersal via birds and small mammals, who found the olive fruit to be a much-appreciated replacement for their lost native food sources. Sources that had disappeared due to poor land management and clearing by the colonisers.

The natural range of the native olive, *Olea paniculata*, is in tropical eastern Australia, from northern New South Wales all the way to Cape York. The native olive has small, edible black berries (i.e. olives) similar to those of its wild European and African relatives, but its leaves are wider as opposed to elongated in shape, and the tree grows sparsely branched and up to 30 metres tall.

The introduced *Olea europaea* and subspecies can now be found from southern Queensland to Perth, with massive populations in greater Sydney and the Adelaide Hills. In some regions, legislation has been passed declaring wild olives as priority noxious weeds, to be controlled on both government and private land. In New South Wales alone, the government and land managers spend millions trying to contain this tree.

I, however, see this as a missed opportunity to utilise available food and medicinal resources, in particular the manufacture of olive leaf extract, which we currently import as a high-value product.

Furthermore, talk to any wood turner and they will tell you how much they'd like to put their hands on a good-sized piece of wild olive timber, as it is very hard, heavy, beautifully grained, takes a fine polish and is slightly fragrant. A spoon-maker friend of mine loves it so much that whenever an infestation of wild olives is being bulldozed, he runs around picking up the branches to stock up for his passion project.

Fig. 1 *Olea europaea* subsp. *cuspidata*

IDENTIFICATION

Leaves (Fig. 1, i)

The two types of exotic wild olives are easy to distinguish by comparing their leaves. Wild European olives have a grey-green upper leaf and lighter yellow-green underleaf. Wild African olives have a dark green upper leaf, light green underleaf and a very distinctive feature: the very tip of the leaf has a tiny 'hook'. Both species' leaves are elongated, lance-like, 1–2 centimetres wide and up to 8 centimetres long.

Flowers and fruit (Fig. 1, ii)

The flowers appear mainly in spring in clusters at the end of the branches. They have four white to light-cream petals and are about 3–5 millimetres across. The fruits of wild European olives develop mainly in late summer and are a smaller version of those of the traditional cultivated olives, which are elongated, light green maturing to a dark red-brown, and up to 30 millimetres long. Wild African olives' fruits are even smaller and rounder, only about 10–12 millimetres across.

For the forager, the main issue with the fruit of the uncultivated species is size – these trees only produce small fruits in unreliable quantities.

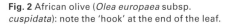

Fig. 2 African olive (*Olea europaea* subsp. *cuspidata*): note the 'hook' at the end of the leaf.

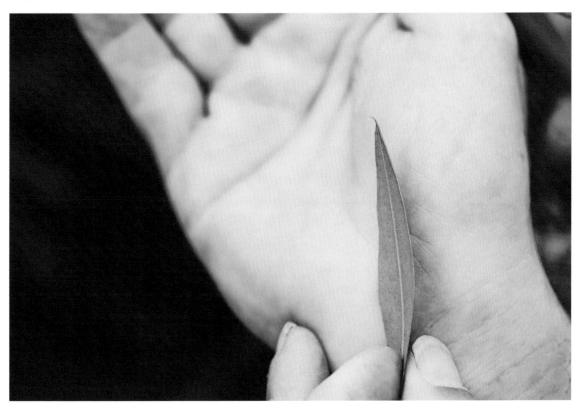

Fig. 3 African olive (*Olea europaea* subsp. *cuspidata*): this tree only offers small berries.

AS FOOD

Wild olives are edible after curing. They are, basically, the feral version of commercial olives (indeed, they are each a subspecies) and carry the same characteristics and medicinal benefits. The fruits are usually pickled or cured with water, salt or lye. They can also be dried in the sun and eaten without curing. The cured fruits can be eaten as a snack or as a relish, or used in breads, soups and salads.

A talented barman friend of mine harvests the fruit to make a tincture for dirty martinis. Now that's a good way to deal with a 'problematic' invasive plant!

If you do not mind some bitterness, you should also try the fully ripe fruits straight from the tree: bitter and sweet at the same time.

AS MEDICINE

Olives are renowned as a healthy food, providing a good source of vitamin E, iron, copper and calcium. The oil obtained from the fruits is rich in mono-unsaturated fats and has been proven to assist in reducing inflammation and lowering the risk of heart disease.

The leaves, though, are the main carriers of health benefits. Employed as an immune-system booster, olive leaf extract helps in the relief of colds, flus and fevers. Use of this remedy has been documented as far back as the ancient Egyptians.

I extract the health benefits of the leaves in my own kitchen, for free, by making the following tea.

Makes 4 cups of tea

Wild olive leaf tea

INGREDIENTS

½ cup wild olive leaves per 1 L boiling water
(*leaves can be used either fresh or dried*)

We make this tea on a regular basis in our house, especially during cold and flu season. When consumed at the first signs of a cold it will help to significantly reduce symptoms – and the medicinal properties of olive leaf will drastically reduce your chances of getting a cold in the first place.

1. Place fresh or dried olive leaves at the bottom of your teapot, or in the leaf basket if it has one.

2. Fill the teapot with boiling water and allow to sit for at least 10 minutes.

3. Pour the tea into your favourite cup and add a spoonful of honey to taste, if desired.

Native figs

EDIBLE PARTS

fruit

SNAPSHOT

Figs are generally enormous trees, growing to a very advanced age and amazing proportions, providing a vital food source and habitat for wildlife. Many of them have aerial roots that grow down into the ground, eventually thickening up and forming 'buttresses'. They are commonly planted in parks and found in old gardens, and because they are all edible, they are an easily foraged plant for beginners.

Marnee, my wife, has fond childhood memories of playing among the oversized root systems of the enormous fig trees of Sydney. As she played, the spaces among the buttress roots transformed into a room in a big tree house or a shop at a market, where the tree's fruits would become currency or produce to sell. The size and age of these trees are such that they have become landmarks and memory points. Found in all Australian states and territories, native figs are an extremely important species in Aboriginal Australian culture, for food, shelter and placemaking.

Fig trees are a large genus of about 750 species (including the renowned commercial fig, *Ficus carica*), of which about fifty are native to Australia. They all have edible fruits – although not all are tasty. Native Australian figs are mostly found in the tropics, but there are about six species that are common further south. Of those, the best edibles are the sandpaper fig (*Ficus coronata*), the white sandpaper fig (*Ficus fraseri*), the Port Jackson fig (*Ficus rubiginosa*), the Moreton Bay fig (*Ficus macrophylla*) – pictured opposite – and the strangler fig (*Ficus superba* var. *henneana*).

IDENTIFICATION

Leaves (Fig. 1, i)

The leaves range from small to quite wide, but all have a waxy appearance and a sticky latex sap that oozes out of any damaged part of the tree, including the leaves and stems.

Flowers and fruit (Fig. 1, ii)

Figs are unique, as their flowers are located inside their fruit and can only be pollinated by specific wasps in a co-dependent relationship. The fruits form during the warm months, but it is quite common to see fully ripened fruits throughout the year.

AS FOOD

I often snack on the fruit, and by now have my favourite trees. Our Australian varieties can range from sweet and juicy to rather dry and bland. Let your own sense of taste guide you to finding your favourite tree. The trick is to harvest the fruit when it is fully ripe, then check the fruit for bugs, and enjoy!

Fig. 1 *Ficus rubiginosa*

Fig. 2 Unripe fruits of the Port Jackson fig (*Ficus rubiginosa*).

Fig. 3 Native figs (*Ficus* species): the big one is a Moreton Bay fig (*Ficus macrophylla*), while the others are Port Jackson figs (*Ficus rubiginosa*) in various stages of ripenes.

Blackberry

SNAPSHOT

The blackberry is a semi-deciduous scrambler, meaning it loses its leaves every year. However, by the time the last of the season's leaves are gone, the new ones are already forming, so you will never see a bush without some foliage.

It forms thick, thorny bushes up to 2 metres in height, with branches (canes) extending to about 7 metres in length. There are many varieties and microspecies of blackberries in Australia, and scientists refer to them collectively as '*Rubus fruticosus* aggregate'.

Please note that this is a restricted species and is therefore often poisoned. Make sure you know your local colonies and how they have been managed. Also be careful of the thorns!

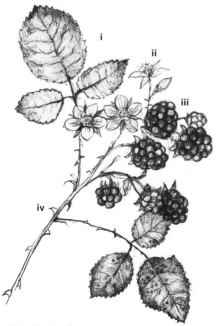

Fig. 1 *Rubus fruticosus*

Blackberry foraging is one of the most straightforward, wild-food gathering activities and is available in a wide variety of environments. These plants are easy to recognise and relatively simple to harvest (apart from the thorns) – and when you find the right bush, they are just delicious!

The thorns can be painful and boring, clinging on to your clothes; if you're not careful, they can cause injuries, bad scratches in particular. In my opinion, the best way to harvest these fruits is by slowing down – if you're too hasty you get caught in the branches.

The blackberry is so common that it has been declared a Weed of National Significance for its adverse impact on agriculture, tourism and native ecologies. For that reason, blackberry bushes are often sprayed with herbicides, particularly when growing along roadsides and in agricultural settings. Please make sure you know your local colony has not been poisoned before harvesting.

IDENTIFICATION

Leaves and canes (Fig. 1, i, iv)

The leaves are usually made up of three or five egg-shaped leaflets. They can vary in size from 3–9 centimetres long and 2–5 centimetres wide, and are dark green on the upper surface and lighter underneath.

The ribbed canes start off green when young and turn reddish or purple with age. Blackberry thorns are straight or curved and appear along the entire length of the canes.

Flowers and fruit (Fig. 1, ii, iii)

In spring and summer, white or pink flowers appear, up to 3 centimetres wide and comprising five petals. The size of the fruit varies from 1–3 centimetres across; initially green, it ripens through red to black. The fruit is made up of several juicy berries, each with a 1–2 millimetre seed inside.

AS FOOD

The trick to foraging for blackberries is to find a good colony. I have never found excellent bushes around Sydney – here they never mature into a sweet treat – but down south in Victoria and Tasmania you can get some excellent juicy, sweet, fruity harvests. There are lots of varieties and subspecies, so the flavour and fleshiness of the fruits varies a lot from plant to plant. The best bushes produce juicy berries for several months, from November to April. The fruits can be preserved as syrups, jams and jellies, while the young leaves are widely used in herbal tea blends, adding a fruity flavour.

Acetosa sagittata

Rambling dock

EDIBLE PARTS

leaf, shoot

SNAPSHOT

Rambling dock is a climber that 'rambles' over other bushes and plants. It is regarded as a perennial plant, as it has the ability to create underground tubers, from which it can reshoot if the aboveground growth dies off due to frost or drought (or human attempts at eradication). It produces long runners, up to 2 metres in length. Each runner has several branches, which act like ladders, allowing the plant to overcome other vegetation when competing for sunlight. Rambling dock is a striking plant, and once you recognise its features you can easily spot it from quite a distance.

Rambling dock is one of the most popular of the wild greens that I provide to restaurants and bars – its juicy, sour, fresh flavour makes it a standout ingredient in salads and cocktails. This plant grows absolutely everywhere along the coastal fringes of south-eastern Australia, and at any time of the year you are bound to find some juicy young leaves.

If you're interested in this plant, do consider joining your local bush regeneration group, as they will no doubt direct you to several 'infestations'; they will also give you a big bag that you can fill with as much rambling dock as you like.

IDENTIFICATION

Leaves and stalks (Fig. 1, i)

The leaves are the most readily recognisable feature of the plant: they grow in an alternate arrangement along the stems and have a peculiar arrowhead shape. They are 6–10 centimetres long and 3–5 centimetres wide. The stems, which are ribbed, start off green, turning red as they age or when stressed due to cold weather or lack of water.

Flowers and seeds

The flowers are small and green to off-white, growing in grape-like clusters. They develop into three-winged paper-like seed pods, which are green at first, before turning red and finally cream-white when fully mature.

Fig. 1 *Acetosa sagittata*

Fig. 2 Rambling dock (*Acetosa sagittata*), easily recognisable by the arrow-shaped leaves.

AS FOOD

The leaves and young shoots have a sharp, lemon-sherbet-like flavour that always surprises people when they first encounter it. It's like sucking on a lemon, but with the higher acidity notes of sorrel (*Rumex acetosa*).

The leaves can be cooked, and although they lose some sharpness and colour in the process, they transform into a pleasant, silky-textured vegetable with a sweet-sour flavour. In Indonesia the leaves are used in place of tamarind, and are baked with fish.

I love them best raw in salsa verde (see below for a recipe) or in fresh salads, for example Vietnamese-style noodle salads, with chilli and bitter greens such as dandelion or sow thistle.

Rambling dock is a very popular garnish for cocktails, particularly gin-based ones, offering not only a sharpness that balances the gin's tannins and tonic water's bitter tones, but also an interesting, bright-green visual feature for the drink's presentation.

I always de-stem the leaves before using them in the kitchen, as the stems can be a bit woody.

During a series of TEDx talks in Sydney in 2015, I provided ingredients for the catering. The theme for the three-day event's menu was Rebel Food. For this occasion I was working with the (at the time) head chef of ARIA catering, Sarah Jewell. She created an incredibly simple yet perfect salad of carrot peelings with rambling dock leaves, bringing together a deep-orange, sweet and earthy by-product of catering, and a bright-green, sharp and crunchy weed. Delicious. I still talk about it.

Makes about 8 servings

Three-weed salsa verde

The tangy lemon flavour of rambling dock is perfectly suited to this recipe, which is an adaptation of my mum's original. It can be served as a dipping sauce, condiment or marinade.

INGREDIENTS

2 cups rambling dock leaves

½ cup cobbler's pegs leaves

½ cup dandelion leaves

1 cup parsley leaves

2 garlic cloves, crushed

2 tbsp capers, drained

½ cup extra virgin olive oil

A dash of red wine vinegar

1 tsp Dijon mustard

Juice of 1 lemon

Sea salt and pepper to taste

1. Place the rambling dock, cobbler's pegs, dandelion, parsley, garlic and capers in a food processor. Process until finely chopped.

2. With the motor running, add oil, vinegar, mustard and lemon juice to the mixture. Process until well combined.

3. Season with sea salt and pepper. Let stand for 10 minutes before serving.

Commelina cyanea

Scurvy weed

SNAPSHOT

Scurvy weed is a low, sprawling, ground-covering plant, usually found in moist areas under the shade of trees. It is an evergreen, forming dense mats of delicate and fleshy runners, often rooting from the branching joints. The plant can spread for 3–5 metres, or even further in the right conditions, and is dotted with bright-blue flowers in the warmer months.

Scurvy weed was given its common name by Sydney's early colonists, who used to eat a lot of this plant, raw and cooked, trying to compensate for the lack of vitamin C in their diet.

Despite its rather gloomy place in Australia's European history, scurvy weed – a common creeping ground cover, native to New South Wales and Queensland – is a colourful, easily recognisable plant that makes a fair foraged meal.

Scurvy weed is native and should not be confused with the common, exotic yet naturalised, 'trad' – *Tradescantia* species. Trad is similar in its growth behaviour and can be found in similar locations, but it has a white flower.

IDENTIFICATION

Leaves and stalks (Fig. 1, ii)

The leaves are bright green, measuring up to 7 centimetres long and resembling a miniature sword in shape. The stems are knotted at the joints and can readily root from there. Any small length of the stem can take hold in a new location, spreading easily via vegetative propagation.

Flowers and seeds (Fig. 1, i)

The flowers are the distinctive feature of the plant, with three equally sized, bright-blue petals. The seeds are formed in a cream-white capsule and are 2–3 millimetres wide.

AS FOOD

Scurvy weed is a green vegetable with leaves that have a taste and texture similar to that of baby spinach. I cook it in soups and pies or use it fresh in smoothies and salads. The flowers can be added to both savoury and sweet dishes as a colourful garnish.

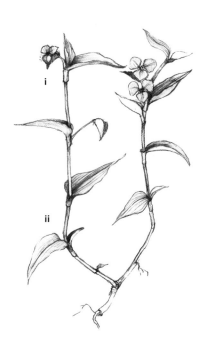

Fig. 1 *Commelina cyanea*

Fig. 2 Scurvy weed (*Commelina cyanea*) leaves.

Fig. 3 Scurvy weed (*Commelina cyanea*) typical blue flower.

Chapter 03

✳   This chapter will focus on seaside ecologies, showcasing indigenous and exotic species. These form the basis for discussing how we relate to the sea and how this relationship can inform our connection to country.

Sea

Sea

Sun-kissed, salty skin and getting sand in places you'd rather not. A soundscape of waves, seabirds and play. The beach is an access point to the vast wilderness that is the ocean.

The vast majority of Australians live within 100 kilometres of the sea. For many of us, it represents an easily tapped memory bank full of beachside holidays, surfing, swimming, sunbaking and seashell collecting.

A great mate and foraging colleague of mine, Oliver Brown, says that an outing at the beach should be more than a dip in the water: we should cultivate the childhood curiosity that entertained us for hours around a rockpool when we were kids - discovery sessions that were so important in informing how we came to value and appreciate nature and natural processes.

There is something magical about the feeling of connection to a place. Through simple engagement with your local natural environment, you enact an ancient ritual of care. By getting to know the plants of your locale, you foster a process of belonging. You become a stakeholder, which enables you to nurture your role as caretaker.

And a great example of this is foraging on and by the beach.

Seaside legalities and ethics

The specifics of coastal ecology regulations vary from state to state. You also need to be aware that legislations change and the boundaries of protected areas shift. The range of permissions varies from being completely unregulated outside of marine reserves or national parks, to a clearly defined limit for personal use, to the need for a harvesting licence. Please consult with your local council with regard to your current regulations.

As a general rule, never pull seaweeds from their 'holdfast'. The holdfast is the root-like structure at the base of seaweeds that anchors them to a stable surface, such as rock or the seabed. (Seaweeds do not have a root system, as they take up nutrients from seawater through their fronds.) Instead, harvest by cutting, leaving behind the holdfast so that the seaweed can regenerate – or better still, collect seaweed when it has washed ashore.

Please note that seaweeds are important not only when they are alive in the water, but also when they are decaying on the beach. They are a vital element in marine ecosystems, existing at the lower level of the food web. Fish, birds, snails, crabs and marine mammals use kelp beds for food, refuge or spawning, or as nursery grounds. Kelp beds also trap and stabilise sediment, and disperse wave energy and turbulence, in this way protecting beaches from erosion.

For this reason it is advisable that you do not harvest seaweed from the sea, but rather wait for it to float freely.

Finally, please be aware that it is best not to harvest from the beach straight after a storm. Particularly in built-up environments, storm channels will carry the debris of the city to the shore, polluting the water and everything in it.

Previous spread, left Neptune's pearls (*Hormosira banksii*) floating in the water.

'As an Aboriginal cultural heritage consultant, I work under the premise shared with Aboriginal people that the cultural significance of places can be found through understanding Connection to Country, and that Connection to Country is articulated through stories. All around Australia these include the experiences of those who define themselves as Saltwater People, whose stories and identity are intertwined with the ocean. There is something special about the way the ocean so fully captivates those who engage with it. There are those who swim, surf, dive, sail, fish or even just come to be near it without getting wet. For those of us who are coastal foragers, that engagement is made all the deeper with being literally, physically sustained by the environment of the sea and its shores. It changes not just us, but our perception of the place with us as a component.'

— Oliver Brown, Sydney-based forager and archaeologist

Ecklonia radiata

Golden kelp

EDIBLE PARTS

frond

SNAPSHOT

Golden kelp is a large brown or golden-brown seaweed that grows up to 1.5 metres long, with frilled fronds branching out from a flat, wide midrib. At the base of the stem is the holdfast, which looks like the roots of a tree but is actually an anchoring structure that holds the seaweed in place.

Golden kelp can be found on the shores of Brisbane, and all the way along the coast down to Melbourne and Adelaide, and then around to Perth and Geraldton in Western Australia.

You will find it washed up on the beach in big piles after rough seas, mixed up with debris and other seaweeds. The best time to harvest golden kelp is just after high tide: as the sea recedes, it leaves the fresh seaweed behind on the sand. After its holdfast has become detached from the sea floor, kelp will remain alive even when floating freely in the sea. Its fronds (the equivalent of leaves in a plant) continue to photosynthesise, using energy from the sun and absorbing nutrients from the water. Kelp will not stay fresh on the beach forever, though. That's why I collect it immediately after high tide, to minimise the time the seaweed sits in the sun, potentially rotting away.

IDENTIFICATION

Fronds (Fig. 1, i)

Golden kelp's midrib (Fig. 1, ii) starts from the holdfast as a round 'stalk' 1–2 centimetres thick, which flattens out to 5–15 millimetres thick and 30–100 millimetres wide, thinning out at the top. Several frilled and wavy fronds (Fig. 1, i) branch out from the midrib. These irregularly shaped fronds are only a few millimetres thick, 30–80 millimetres wide and 50–200 millimetres long, and often encrusted with microalgae.

AS FOOD

I love golden kelp in pickles, and on the following page I share my recipe for it – simple, delicious, universal and suitable for a number of seaweeds (for example, Neptune's pearls, p. 128). The result is never the same: the seaweed species change, and the amount of vinegar used is sometimes more, sometimes less. At times I also put a teaspoon of sugar in with it. This is just a guide – make this recipe your own.

For pickling I only use the midrib, as it is easier to clean and process, but I have friends who collect the side fronds and use them in udon soups, cooking them with the noodles. Being thinner than the midrib, the fronds can provide an excellent bitey texture to the soup, adding a salty, umami flavour.

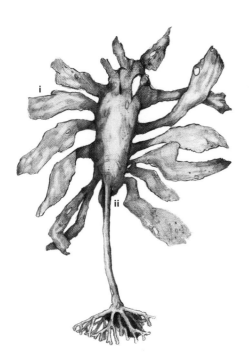

Fig. 1 *Ecklonia radiata*

Seaweed pickle

INGREDIENTS

2 clumps golden kelp

1 cup white vinegar

Salt

Spices to season, such as coriander seeds and black peppercorns

1. Cut off the frilly bits from your kelp fronds, leaving only the central midribs.

2. Add 3 cups of water to a saucepan and bring to the boil. Add the kelp and boil for about 1 minute.

3. Once it is cool enough to handle, trim the blanched seaweed into matchstick- or fettucine-width pieces, depending on how thick you want them, and place the pieces in your sterilised jars (see p. 52).

4. Add the vinegar and 1 cup of water to a saucepan and bring to the boil.

5. Add a couple of pinches of salt, a few black peppercorns (if using) and a pinch of each of your chosen spices.

6. Pour the hot pickling liquid into your jars, making sure the seaweed is completely covered. The liquid should reach 1–2 centimetres from the rim of the jar and fully cover the seaweed. You may need to top up the liquid. Allow the jars to stand for a few minutes.

7. Seal and label the jars, including the date made. To check that your jars are well sealed, while they are still warm turn them upside down for a few minutes.

8. This pickle keeps for up to a year stored in a cool, dry place away from sunlight. Once opened, it should be kept in the fridge, and will last for up to a month.

Ulva lactuca

Sea lettuce

EDIBLE PARTS

frond

SNAPSHOT

Sea lettuce is a thin, flat, green seaweed growing from a round holdfast, forming expansive mats several metres wide. The frond resembles a leaf of lettuce. You will find big colonies of this seaweed growing closely together in rockpools or on flat rock platforms that are regularly washed by waves.

Sea lettuce is a cosmopolitan seaweed, growing all over the world. It is found all around Australia on rock platforms in the intertidal zone, the part of the seashore that is above water level at low tide and underwater at high tide. You will need to look for sea lettuce at low tide.

In Australia it is much appreciated by fishers, who use it as bait for blackfish (luderick).

Always be careful where you harvest your sea lettuce, making sure that the surrounding area is clean and has a great tidal exchange and fast currents. Always be sure to cut the sea lettuce fronds, leaving the holdfast behind to regenerate.

IDENTIFICATION

Fronds (Fig. 1, i)

The margins of sea lettuce fronds are somewhat ruffled and are often torn. Fronds may reach 18 centimetres in length and up to 30 centimetres across, though generally they are much shorter. Translucent, and green to dark green in colour, the fronds turn white or black when dry or dead.

AS FOOD

Like lettuce grown on land, sea lettuce can be used raw in salads. It can also be cooked and added to soups. I like to quickly sauté sea lettuce with sesame oil and a dash of lime juice, roll it in rice paper with sliced cucumber and rice noodles, and then serve it with a peanut sauce. On the following page I give a version of this recipe featuring macadamias and sweet chilli sauce.

AS MEDICINE

Sea lettuce is an amazing source of nutrients. It is made up of 28 per cent protein, comprising all nine essential amino acids, including lysine, which is often lacking in a vegetarian diet. The pigments found in this seaweed have a high concentration of chlorophyll, as well as strong antioxidant properties.

i

Fig. 1 *Ulva lactuca*

Sea lettuce and macadamia rice-paper rolls

INGREDIENTS

60 g rice vermicelli or rice noodles

2 cups sea lettuce, washed and chopped

2 tbsp fresh lime juice

1 tbsp sesame oil

½ cup roasted and roughly chopped macadamias

2 large iceberg lettuce leaves, finely chopped

1 tbsp sweet chilli sauce – plus extra, to serve

8 rice-paper wrappers

An Australian seaside twist to an Asian fast-food favourite. These rolls are healthy, fresh and fun to make with kids. Set up a rolling station and away you go. They allow plenty of room to create your own version with things like avocado strips, julienne vegetables and grilled tofu.

1. Bring a medium saucepan of water to the boil. Add the rice noodles and boil for 3–5 minutes, or until al dente, then drain. Rinse thoroughly with cold water so the noodles don't stick together. Leave them to cool.

2. Clean the sea lettuce of any sand or sea life, trim into smallish pieces and sauté in a shallow pan with the lime juice and sesame oil until it becomes soft. Set aside and allow to cool.

3. Mix all the ingredients, except the rice-paper wrappers, in a large bowl.

4. Fill a large shallow bowl with hot water. Place a wet tea towel on the work surface nearby. Dip one wrapper into the water for 10 seconds to soften. Lay the wrapper on the wet tea towel and place a handful of the noodle mix across the centre, leaving about 5 cm of the wrapper uncovered on each side.

5. Fold the uncovered sides of the wrapper inwards, then tightly roll to enclose the filling. Repeat with the remaining rolls.

6. Serve fresh with sweet chilli sauce.

Fig. 2 Sea lettuce (*Ulva lactuca*) and Neptune's pearls (*Hormosira banksii*) fresh from the surf.

Codium fragile

Deadman's fingers

EDIBLE PARTS

frond

SNAPSHOT

This seaweed grows in isolated 'bushes' down to 2 metres below sea level, in the intertidal and subtidal zone. As it sways in the water, it really conjures the macabre vision of drowned fleshy fingers waving with the motion of the sea.

Deadman's fingers. An unforgettable name for such a common seaweed. There are several subspecies, including native versions, and it is now extending its range and becoming invasive worldwide. Here in Australia it can be found on the coast of New South Wales, Tasmania, Victoria and South Australia.

It is best to collect fresh fronds at low tide and to use them within the day. Please harvest responsibly by cutting the fronds off and leaving the holdfast behind, so the seaweed can continue to grow.

IDENTIFICATION

Fronds (Fig. 1, i)

The branched 'fingers' can be 5–10 millimetres wide and up to 30 centimetres long. They are deep green when in water but very quickly turn dark green/black when out of it. At low tide, the fronds droop down just like floppy fingers. The whole plant is slimy, with a distinctive velvety feel due to very fine, tubular microhairs coating the surface.

AS FOOD

Much appreciated for its nutritional value (proteins, minerals and fibre), deadman's fingers is farmed in Korea, where it is used raw in seaweed salads or as a side dish. The flavour is very seafood-like: think of fresh oysters or mussels as a comparison. If you want to cook it, do so quickly and gently, as it breaks down into mush rather quickly. Most chefs use it raw.

The fronds have a velvety texture, which can be an unusual and therefore challenging experience for some; this can be masked with other ingredients, like potatoes or tomatoes.

Fig. 1 _Codium fragile_

Hormosira banksii

Neptune's pearls

EDIBLE PARTS

bead

SNAPSHOT

Neptune's pearls features green-brown fronds that each resemble a string of beads held together by short, thin segments of stalk. The strings of 'pearls' radiate from a central holdfast.

Neptune's pearls or Neptune's necklace is a common seaweed found in rockpools and rock platforms in many Australian states. It grows abundantly from the south of Port Macquarie in New South Wales all the way around to Western Australia.

This seaweed lives in the intertidal zone, at times forming big mats and creating an important microhabitat for small crustaceans, molluscs, worms and fish, which eat this seaweed and use it to shelter in.

It is common to see dislodged fronds floating in the water, and many kids use the distinctive beads as ammunition in battle games.

IDENTIFICATION

Fronds (Fig. 1, i)

The fronds can grow to a length of 30 centimetres. The hollow, round or oval-shaped 'pearls' (vesicles) are up to 1.5 centimetres in diameter and filled with water, in this way preventing the seaweed drying out when it's not covered by water. The fronds are light green to dark brown and usually blemished by little clumps and irregularities; they are often slimy, another way of preserving moisture when they are exposed to the sun.

AS FOOD

Neptune's pearls will deteriorate quite quickly once picked; this seaweed should be eaten or processed on the same day it is harvested. Refrigeration in brine will assist in keeping it a bit longer: quite simply, collect a bucket of seawater to hold the seaweed while it's in the fridge.

I eat Neptune's pearls raw when it's fresh and crunchy – to me it resembles a brined olive in taste and texture. The drop of salty water inside each bead gives it a distinctive flavour of the sea. It also makes for an excellent pickle (see recipe on p. 120).

i

Fig. 1 *Hormosira banksii*

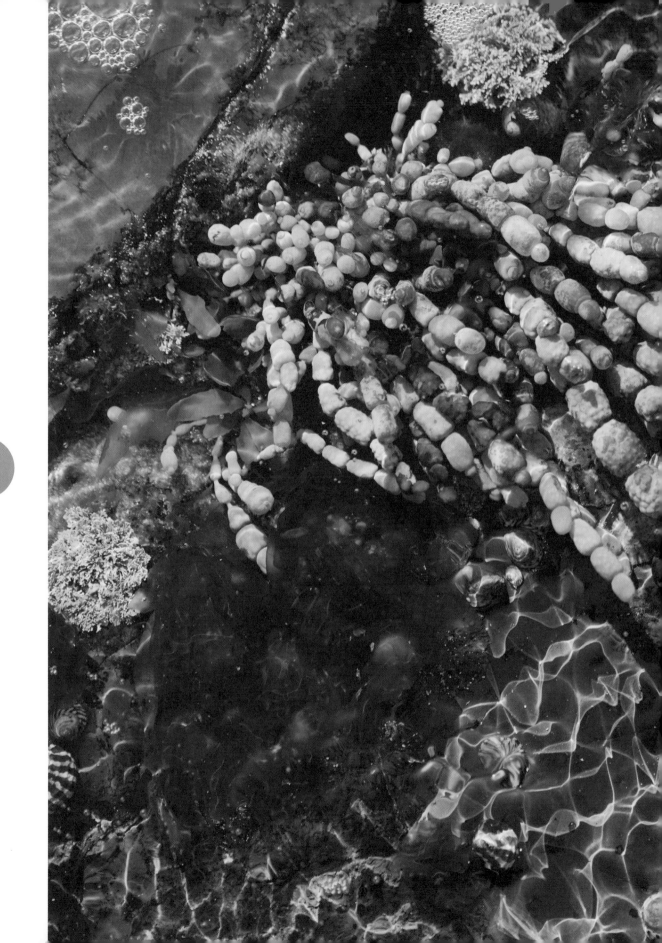

Carpobrotus species

Pigface

EDIBLE PARTS

leaf, fruit

SNAPSHOT

Pigface grows as a mat of fleshy, finger-like leaves. With its long and branched runners, it is an important dune stabiliser, holding the sand in place and creating organic matter despite the salty and windy conditions. It can spread extensively, to a width of several metres.

Pigface is an easily identifiable coastal plant, found all around Australia. We have about a handful of species, all of them edible, with varying degrees of palatability.

The more widespread species are *Carpobrotus rossii*, a native found on the coast of Victoria, Tasmania, South Australia and Western Australia; *Carpobrotus glaucescens* (pictured opposite), native, found on the east coast from Townsville to Melbourne; *Carpobrotus edulis* and *Carpobrotus aequilaterus*, both exotics, found from north of Brisbane all the way around to Perth; and *Carpobrotus modestus*, native, found in Victoria, South Australia and Western Australia.

You will mostly find pigface scrambling over dunes and overhanging rock platforms – apart from *Carpobrotus modestus*, which also grows inland. Pigface grows well above high-tide level and loves full sun. In summer it is constantly covered in daisy-like hot-pink flowers – or light-yellow flowers in the case of *Carpobrotus edulis*. Councils commonly plant it in roundabouts and other street gardens, but those plantings do not have good-tasting fruits. The best varieties are the wild ones growing at the beach.

When it gets too cold or too dry, this plant shrivels away and dies off, only to come back as happy as ever when the conditions improve.

Fig. 1 *Carpobrotus* species

IDENTIFICATION

Leaves and stalks (Fig. 1, ii)

The leaves and stalks are bright, deep green but can turn red when stressed by lack of water or if the weather gets cold. The leaves are 30–100 millimetres long and 8–15 millimetres wide, shaped like a finger, but with the distinctive feature of being triangular in cross-section. Pigface is in leaf all year round.

Flowers, fruit and seeds (Fig. 1, i)

The flowers are big and showy, up to 70 millimetres wide, with hot-pink or shiny yellow petals circling a light-yellow centre. Fruits will grow once the flower is spent, forming a horned capsule that turns red when mature. Peel off the skin and you will reveal soft white flesh filled with tiny seeds. Pigface usually flowers from September to April and fruits from November to April. Often the plant has flowers that do not produce fruit.

AS FOOD

Pigface is best known for its fruits. I love to harvest these when I'm at the beach, while my feet are still wet, and eat them on the spot. I collect a fully ripened fruit (easy to recognise, as it is bright purple-red) and peel off the skin from the base upwards. Inside there is a kiwifruit-like pulp. That pulp is amazing: sweet and salty and juicy. It is truly a revelation.

Please note that not all colonies have great fruits, particularly the bushes planted by councils and bush regenerators, as they are bred asexually and lose their good flavours in exchange for adaptability.

You can also eat the leaves, but some species (like *Carpobrotus glaucescens* and *Carpobrotus rossii*) taste better than others. Pigface fruits and leaves have been used by Aboriginal Australians as a food source and are now part of the revival of bush tucker.

Some of my friends cold-press the leaves to obtain a salty and astringent juice, excellent in gin-based cocktails.

AS MEDICINE

Traditionally, the crushed leaves are used to alleviate insect bites, skin irritations and mild burns.

Lomandra species

Mat rush

EDIBLE PARTS

leaf, flower, seed

SNAPSHOT

Mat rush forms spiky, semi-spherical bushes, 0.5–1.5 metres tall and wide. The plant is a perennial and keeps growing from year to year from a crowded root clump. It can survive severe pruning, and even fires, by regenerating from the root clumps.

Mat rush has many ornamental cultivars and is used extensively as a street and garden landscaping plant in Australia and overseas. Aboriginal people have traditionally used the species as a reliable food source, and for weaving into mats and dillybags. We recognise about fifty species in Australia, all of them native, spread out across the continent, including the tropics and the inland deserts. They are generally small bushes with long, narrow leaves extending from a central core, ranging from 20–30 centimetres to 1.5 metres in height. The most common species are *Lomandra filiformis* and *Lomandra multiflora* – found all over Queensland, New South Wales, Victoria and South Australia – and *Lomandra longifolia*, also found in Tasmania.

The best way to find out which one grows in your area is by consulting your local native species lists, which you can get from the council.

Fig. 1 *Lomandra* species

Please note that mat rush is a spiky sedge: the leaves have sharp edges and the seed heads have long thorns. Be careful when handling the plant.

Fig. 2 Mat rush (*Lomandra longifolia*) flowering spike.

IDENTIFICATION

Leaves (Fig. 1, ii)

The deep-green leaves are long and narrow, tough but flexible, growing up to 1 metre long by 1 centimetre wide. When stressed by lack of water, they appear to roll inwards. They have sharp edges that can easily cut through your skin if you don't handle them carefully. The leaves form around clusters of shoots growing from a single rootstock.

Flowers and seeds (Fig. 1, i)

Male and female flowers occur on separate plants. The flowers appear in springtime, along flattened flowering branches reaching 30–70 centimetres long. When foraging, please be mindful of the sharp, pointed spikes at the base of each flower. The flowers are tiny, only a few millimetres wide, creamy white in colour and sweetly fragrant. Male flowers will drop soon after pollination, while female plants will develop seeds. The female fruiting spike carries 50–70 round seeds, each one 3–5 millimetres across. You will notice that the seeds are divided into two halves (kernels).

Root

The roots are thick, woody rhizomes that generate long, blade-like leaves. While the roots themselves are very fibrous, the young shoots can be crunchy, juicy and sweet.

AS FOOD

You can eat both the male and female flowers raw. They are sweet and fragrant, resembling peas in flavour. The flowers are easy to harvest if you pull upwards from the base of the branches, caressing the spikes with your hands as you clutch the flowering head.

Another enjoyable part of the plant is the white leaf base. It can be juicy and sweet, resembling sweet corn in flavour. To access the leaf base, you will have to rip a few clumps of leaves from the plant.

The seeds from the female plants are also widely used. Harvested when young and green, they too are juicy and sweet. When they have fully matured into bright-yellow 3–8 millimetre shells, they become hard and require pounding into a paste or flour. Indigenous Australians make damper cakes from the mature seeds of mat rush.

I harvest the seed spike and leave it to rest in the shade. The seed shells will open after a few days and release the kernels, which I first pound in a mortar and pestle and then grind into a flour, mixing it with self-raising flour for baking or using it for pancakes.

Other people sprout the seeds and then add them to soups or have them fresh in salads.

Cakile maritima and *Cakile edentula*

Beach mustard

EDIBLE PARTS

leaf, flower

SNAPSHOT

In simple terms, beach mustard is just like wild mustard (*Brassica* species, see p. 178), but fleshier and saltier. It grows from a central rosette, up to 50 centimetres in height. An annual, it dies off each year after seeding and is one of the few plants that grow in severe coastal conditions, surviving big seas and high salinity.

We have two varieties of beach mustard in Australia, both exotic: *Cakile maritima* (pictured opposite), from Europe, and *Cakile edentula*, from North America. Both are now naturalised along coastal areas of much of Australia, from Mackay in Queensland all the way around to Carnarvon in Western Australia. They are very similar in appearance, and as food can be regarded as interchangeable. Beach mustard is quite widespread and is found on sand dunes and beaches, often forming big colonies.

This plant has a striking spicy-salty taste and is easy to identify due to its striking resemblance to a succulent rocket plant.

IDENTIFICATION

Leaves and stalks (Fig. 1, ii)

The leaves have a variety of forms, from narrow leaflets to quite wide and indented, growing up to 10 centimetres long and 4 centimetres wide. If you are familiar with rocket, you will see the resemblance. The stalks are branched, with leaves and flowers sprouting in the forks. They are up to 8 millimetres thick, and fleshy.

Flowers and seeds (Fig. 1, i)

The flowers are the signature brassica form – with four petals, each 8–14 millimetres long, in a cross-like or 'X' shape. They range from white to pink to light purple in colour. The seeds are also recognisable as those of a brassica, with bean-like seed pods, 10–30 millimetres long, emerging from the flowering stalks and looking like upward-reaching fingers.

AS FOOD

The whole plant is edible, although quite spicy. Leaves are commonly served raw as a peppery garnish (think crunchy, salty wasabi), while the flowers make for an excellent spicy presentation item. I once made a spicy paste by whizzing young leaves in a food processor with a little white vinegar and a touch of salt. We loved it!

Fig. 1 *Cakile maritima* and *Cakile edentula*

Fig. 2 Beach mustard (*Cakile maritima*) growth habit.

Fig. 3 Beach mustard (*Cakile maritima*) typical flower.

Suaeda australis

Seablite

EDIBLE PARTS

leaf

SNAPSHOT

Seablite is a sprawling, fragile-looking bush that grows to 1 metre in height. A short-lived perennial, seablite spreads from the base; its thick, succulent leaves branch outwards, occasionally creating extensive clusters several metres wide.

Seablite is a native Australian coastal bush found in river deltas, around coastal lakes or in salt marshes. There are also a few introduced seablites, but by far the most widespread is the native *Suaeda australis*. It is common to find this plant in combination with other salt-tolerant species such as mangroves, saltbushes and samphire, usually in protected intertidal areas, so please be aware of the local regulations before venturing to harvest this succulent.

IDENTIFICATION

Leaves and stalks (Fig. 1, i)

The leaves are up to 4 centimetres in length and grow thickly on small branches. They are light green to purplish-red in colour. The stalks are wiry (only a few millimetres thick) and fragile, easy to snap at the extremities.

Flowers, fruit and seeds

The minuscule flowers are green-red in colour. They appear from September to December, followed by small, round, red fruit with tiny black seeds.

AS FOOD

Crunchy, salty, juicy, this plant is a treat on the go, and is much esteemed by chefs. I use it fresh in salads, and sometimes dry it by resting the leaves on a paper tray in the shade and forgetting about it. The leaves will eventually crumble into a salty green powder that I use as novelty salt on special dishes like rice-paper rolls.

Fig. 1 *Suaeda australis*

Plantago coronopus

Buck's-horn plantain

SNAPSHOT

Plantago coronopus is a low-growing biennial herb, with a long taproot. It has layered leaves radiating out from the central crown, and a distinctive tall flowering spike. The plant can withstand regular mowing by spreading out, as opposed to growing tall.

Buck's-horn plantain is a common, low-lying herb, which is often found growing as a lawn weed where the grass reaches the beach. Highly salt-tolerant, this plant is an indication of salinity in the soil.

It is cultivated commercially as a vegetable in many parts of the world, including Australia and Italy. Buck's-horn plantain is found wild on the coast of New South Wales, Victoria, Tasmania, South Australia, Western Australia (up to just north of Geraldton) and Queensland (up to just north of Brisbane). It is also common inland in high-salinity regions of New South Wales, Victoria and South Australia. If your grass is dying because of salt, check what's growing on the edges, as it would be buck's-horn plantain surviving the impossible, not the lawn.

IDENTIFICATION

Leaves and stalks (Fig. 1, ii)

Buck's-horn plantain gets its name from the shape of its lobed leaves, which resemble a deer's antlers. The leaves can grow between 6 and 20 centimetres long; although generally green in colour, they can turn red with age. The hairy, leafless stalks emerge from the central crown of the plant and can grow up to 30 centimetres high. There are up to twenty individual flowering stalks on a mature plant.

Flowers and seeds (Fig. 1, i)

The cylinder-shaped flowering body – which resembles a stand-up microphone – grows at the tip of the typical *Plantago* flowering stalk (see plantain, p. 51). The tiny white flowers occur in large numbers, forming a dense swelling at the end of the stalk.

AS FOOD

In Italy, the very young shoots are eaten raw in *misticanza*, a traditional seasonal salad of wild greens. Buck's-horn plantain needs to be picked while young, before the plant flowers, as it becomes bitter and fibrous with age. It is regarded as one of the tastiest plants of the *Plantago* genus. The leaves are crunchy and tender, often salty, with nutty undertones, and they can be blanched in boiling water for a few seconds before serving, in order to soften their texture and reduce bitterness. This plant regularly makes it into my greens crisper. I love it because it can last for a week or more in the fridge, becoming part of the mixed greens I use in sauces, pies, soups, curries or stir-fries. It really is very versatile, an excellent addition to your foraging list.

Fig. 1 *Plantago coronopus*

Chapter 04

✳   Freshwater ecologies are places of great variety, allowing for a seasonal abundance that continues to be exploited by many cultures into the present day. Here, we learn the how-to of gathering foraged food while taking care of our local bushland.

River

River

Soft light skimming over the water at dawn. The call of birds, who take it in turns to fill the still air with their ancient songs. The deep, nutritious soil of alluvial flats, rich and strong in scent and vitality. We are here, at the river.

I grew up by a river and it remains a wondrous environment for me, sparking my imagination and sense of adventure, just as it did when I was a child. Rivers are unpredictable and ever-changing; they move and shift, mutating landscapes, burying valleys and creating swamps. Countless species of plants benefit from the constant availability of water and the occasional floods.

In our cities and suburbs, rivers represent some of the last remaining wildlife corridors and 'wild spaces' - even though many urban waterways have effectively become drainage channels and outflows for storm water, choked with the pollutants produced by city living.

Much of modern foraging happens along rivers and creeks, where migrant communities have long been gathering wild foods. Elderly Chinese women harvesting shepherd's purse greens from floodplains and riverside parks in late winter and early spring, Greek grandmothers collecting wild fennel seeds from the riverbank in autumn - foraging for ingredients for their special dishes, carrying on the traditional practices that connect them with their cultural values.

Foraging today has broadened its reach beyond these old folks' habits, and is now embraced by the young chefs and mixologists who want to bring new flavours to the table and bar. While the old migrants collect exotic weeds, the young chefs tend to go for native species, proposing plants that speak of place and are unique to our shores. Both practices are born out of a need to connect, the act of foraging sparked by a wish to engage with our surroundings as participants.

Riverside legalities and ethics

Rivers and creeks, particularly in urban and suburban environments, are often polluted. If you intend to forage by a freshwater body, it is important to first do some research into conditions in the area. Ideally, your council should be able to provide you with the relevant information, but I have found that by far the easiest and most direct way to discover the lie of the land is by talking to the locals – particularly your area's bush regeneration group. Bush regen in Australia is practised by various local groups made up of caring, proactive residents who regularly gather at various sites in their area (usually on a weekend morning) to pull out weeds and foster native ecologies.

When you join a bush regen group, you gain access to their grassroots knowledge of how the land has been treated, including whether or not any toxins or herbicides are present or have been used in the past. These groups will certainly be able to offer help with plant identification, and they are likely to send you off with bags full of (sometimes edible) invasives.

By working with your neighbours in fostering a corner of the ecology where you live, you will be enacting an important aspect of looking after land. And in return you'll get plenty of delicious weeds to eat.

Yet another benefit of joining your local bush regeneration group is the possibility of bypassing the often multi-layered legal framework around liability and permission. Laws regarding rivers tend to be complex and come with several tiers of management and authority that often overlap. These range from state-level water-catchment authorities to those responsible at local council level for parkland and recreation grounds, to federal-level bodies overseeing hydro infrastructure.

'Learning our local waterways and our local watershed can have a profound effect on how we live and how we experience our ecosystem, in place. It's a deeply practical action, but also one which connects us with space and time and the future and the past. If there's just one thing you do to connect with your local landscape, let it be learning your local watershed. The source to the sink, the from and the to… because when it comes down to it, where do we truly come from, and where do we all go to? The water. Always the water.'

— Kirsten Bradley, co-author (with Nick Ritar) of *Milkwood: Real Skills for Down-to-Earth Living*

Capsella bursa-pastoris

Shepherd's purse

EDIBLE PARTS

leaf, stalk, seed pod, root

SNAPSHOT

Shepherd's purse is an annual plant that grows as a rosette, its leaves radiating out from a central crown. When growing in poor conditions, it reaches 20–30 centimetres in height, while in favourable conditions it can be more than 60 centimetres tall, with leaves as long as 30 centimetres. In New South Wales it produces flowers and seeds all through the cold months of the year and disappears when summer settles in, while further south it flowers in spring and sets seed in summer.

Shepherd's purse is a great plant for beginners, as the peculiar 'heart' shape of the seed pods makes it easy to spot in the landscape.

The name 'shepherd's purse' refers to the seed pod's resemblance to a small, distinctively shaped bag – made from a ram's scrotum – that shepherds once carried with them as they herded their flocks. I know this reference may seem a bit crass, but it is nevertheless effective. You will not be able to un-see this little example of ancient analogy whenever you come across it flapping in the wind. This story represents a memorable moment for many people who come on a foraging tour with me, as I reach into my bag of folklore to give people the tools to remember plants via stories.

Shepherd's purse grows in all states and territories, but is most common in eastern and southern Australia, from the north of Brisbane all the way to Adelaide. It is an extraordinary pioneer plant, growing in a wide variety of conditions, as long as it is not too crowded. Shepherd's purse is one of the first plants to appear when soil is disturbed and is very common around human settlements. It is considered the second most widespread weed in the world.

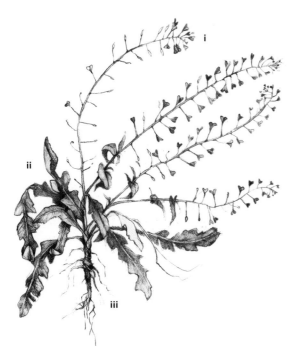

Fig. 1 *Capsella bursa-pastoris*

Please note that shepherd's purse is not a suitable food or medicine for pregnant women.

Fig. 2 Shepherd's purse (*Capsella bursa-pastoris*): when growing in good soil, this plant can exceed 60 centimetres in height.

IDENTIFICATION

Leaves and stalks (Fig. 1, ii)

Shepherd's purse is renowned for its variety of leaf shapes, sometimes deeply toothed, sometimes with irregular jagged edges. The scientific consensus is that all of those different looks are in fact the same plant, which is simply adapting to local conditions. The stalks rise from the centre and have smaller leaves clasping around them at the base, while at the top of the stalk the plant develops its distinctive seed pods.

Flowers and seeds (Fig. 1, i)

Regardless of leaf shape, the flowers will always be the same: white/pink, four petals, up to 3 millimetres wide. And so, importantly, will the seed pods: little green heart-shaped pods branching sideways from a straight stem. The seeds are usually only 1 millimetre long, and light brown.

Root (Fig. 1, iii)

The root is branched, with several thicker rhizomes up to 10 centimetres long. It can grow quite deep and is often fleshy.

AS FOOD

Shepherd's purse is harvested from the wild all over the world. It is also cultivated as a commercial food crop in Asia.

In China it is a commonly used vegetable, particularly in Shanghai and the surrounding region, where it is often stir-fried with rice cakes and other ingredients, or used as part of the filling in wontons. If you go to your local Asian grocery shop and look in the fridge, you're likely to find shepherd's purse dumplings.

In Japan, it is one of the seven herbs used as ingredients for the traditional dish consumed during the springtime festival Nanakusa-no-sekku.

In Korea, it is known as *naengi* and used as a root vegetable in *namul*, side dishes made with fresh greens and wild vegetables.

Shepherd's purse can be eaten raw and has a cabbage-like taste with hints of mustard. I personally love adding the leaves as a green to my casseroles and stir-fries, and I regularly snack on the seed pods while I'm out in the fields.

AS MEDICINE

Shepherd's purse is a very common folk medicine throughout the world, regarded as a remedy to help stop external and internal bleeding. It is used liberally in traditional Chinese medicine to assist with circulation, improve eyesight and regulate blood flow.

Fig. 3 (opposite) The typical tiny flowers and heart-shaped seed pods of shepherd's purse (*Capsella bursa-pastoris*).

Foeniculum vulgare

Wild fennel

EDIBLE PARTS

leaf, stalk, flower, pollen, seed, shoot

SNAPSHOT

Wild fennel is a green, leafy, perennial herb. It can grow up to 2.5 metres high and 1 metre across. Extensive plant colonies – 'fennel forests' – are often seen growing in the wild. The plant is very easy to identify, the key being the scent: unmistakeably aniseed.

Wild fennel is harvested extensively all around the world. It is highly regarded in various cultures for its flavour and beneficial qualities. This is the same species as the fennel you find in the supermarket; however, the latter variety with its swollen bulb has been bred for mass cultivation.

Wild fennel is a master of adaptability, growing proficiently on disturbed land; for example, on the side of the road, on demolition sites or along train lines. It is essential to check whether the area to be harvested has been affected by local pollutants and run-off.

It is quite common to see elderly southern European migrants harvesting this plant from unkempt areas of suburbia. Wild fennel is the classic plant that a Greek *yaya* will make her family stop the car for, before proceeding to harvest it straight from the roadside. In fact, several sources here in Sydney have told me the same story about a *yaya* scolding her fully grown son, employed by the local council, for his part in allowing the local wild fennel colony to be cleared. Is it really that problematic if a corner of the park grows wild fennel? Let the wild plants be part of our landscape, helping to create care and connection.

IDENTIFICATION

Leaves and stalks (Fig. 1, ii)

The leaves have a fine, feathery appearance, and when crushed they also smell like aniseed. They range in length from 5 centimetres up to 20–30 centimetres and always envelop the stalk with a white 'sleeve'. Wild fennel has ribbed stalks that become broader towards the base. Unlike the cultivated variety, this plant does not produce a sizeable bulb.

Flowers and seeds (Fig. 1, i)

Fennel will produce a vibrant display of yellow flower clusters (umbels) in summer, which turn green when transforming into seeds. The individual flowers are only a few millimetres wide, but the size of the umbels can range from a few centimetres to 20 centimetres across.

It is quite common to spot dried-out, light-brown seeds on the plant, as they remain for months after forming. Wild fennel seeds can vary in flavour according to where the plant is growing. Some are sweet, while others can be bitter. Wild fennel is a great example of a plant that should be approached from a caretaker perspective. When you locate a cluster growing in good condition and yielding sweet greens and seeds, look after it, become its caretaker, and the colony will reward you with good-tasting produce forever more.

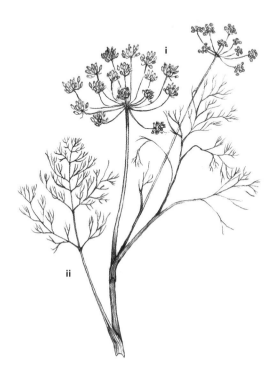

Fig. 1 *Foeniculum vulgare*

Fig. 2 Wild fennel (*Foeniculum vulgare*) seeds.

AS FOOD

All parts of the wild fennel plant are completely edible, from the base to the seeds. Its leaves are best eaten when very young. I love to pull out the new shoots as they form at the nodes of the stalks, peel off the layers to get to the juicy core and enjoy a sweet, crunchy and so delicious wild treat. Older leaves can be used as a garnish or chopped up and cooked with other vegetables.

The aromatic seeds are used as a flavouring in cakes, bread and stuffing mixes. They are commonly used in *mukhwas*, a colourful Indian snack served after a meal to freshen the mouth and aid digestion. They can also be sprouted and added to salads, brewed in refreshing and calming teas, or used as ingredients in cured meats such as Italian salami and sausages.

Fennel pollen is prized by chefs as a garnish, fetching high prices in the hospitality industry.

I mostly use the seeds, which I harvest in autumn/winter and preserve for use throughout the year. They make it into my pickles, soups (see a recipe below) and, occasionally, baked goods.

AS MEDICINE

Fennel as medicine has a long history. Revered worldwide, it is most commonly used as a calming tea for complaints to do with the digestive system. Although the entire plant can be used in various remedies, the seeds are the most medicinally active part. Used as a tea, it is also a known remedy when infants are suffering with colic.

I make a tea with the seeds when I, or my loved ones, suffer from indigestion. Lightly crush the seeds in a mortar to crack the casing, and then add a teaspoon of the crushed seeds to a teapot of boiling water. Let the tea rest for five minutes and serve tepid.

Serves 6

Wild fennel seed and pumpkin soup

INGREDIENTS

1 whole butternut pumpkin, de-skinned and chopped into small chunks

1 brown onion, chopped

1 L chicken-style liquid stock (*we use an organic, vegan, 'chicken' style stock as it gives the soup a very rich flavour*)

2 tbsp wild fennel seeds

250 ml sour cream (*leave out for vegan*)

Salt and pepper to taste

Fresh fennel shoots or flowers for garnish, if available

1. Place the pumpkin, onion and stock in a large pot and cover with enough water to just submerge all the pumpkin chunks.

2. Bring to the boil, then add the fennel seeds.

3. Simmer on low heat until the pumpkin is very soft.

4. Add sour cream, season with salt and pepper, then blend with a stick mixer.

5. Garnish with fresh fennel shoots or flowers if available. Store for up to 3 days in the fridge or freeze for up to 3 months in a sealed container.

Tetragonia species

Native spinach

EDIBLE PARTS

leaf, stalk

SNAPSHOT

Native spinach is a perennial herb, with creeping stems that spread along the ground and branch out at nodes. The plant continues to expand year after year, forming large areas of leafy, exclusive growth up to several metres wide.

Please note that native spinach contains medium levels of oxalic acid and should be blanched in boiling water for 10–15 seconds before consumption. Blanching the leaves in hot water, then rinsing them in cold water and cooking them, reduces the levels of oxalates present. (See wood sorrel, p. 58, for further information.)

Fig. 1 *Tetragonia tetragonioides*

Native spinach (aka warrigal greens, New Zealand spinach, Botany Bay spinach and bower spinach) has become one of Australia's most celebrated edible indigenous species.

As a wild foraged ingredient, native spinach is very easy to recognise, and it can cope with, or even benefit from, low-level tip pruning. By harvesting 10 centimetres off the tips of the branches that you will find growing along the ground, you are promoting new growth. Today, native spinach is cultivated as a vegetable, and is stocked by many local greengrocers.

There are two main varieties of native spinach: warrigals, *Tetragonia tetragonioides*, which grow from Queensland to Victoria, including inland; and bower spinach (*Tetragonia implexicoma*), which is mostly coastal, found growing from eastern Victoria all the way to Western Australia. Both species are edible, and interchangeable for culinary purposes.

Here in Australia, native spinach owes its celebrity status to Captain Cook, who collected it on his voyage to the southern seas in 1770. The *Endeavour*'s botanist, Joseph Banks, took some seeds back to Kew Gardens in England, and in the 19th century native spinach for a time became popular in the UK and Europe as a novelty vegetable. It is now all but forgotten there, except in a few areas of France, where it is still extensively cultivated.

For Australia's early European colonists, native spinach became a much-celebrated food, used as a spinach substitute to alleviate the onset of scurvy in a time and place where traditional European green vegetables were scarce. By contrast, Aboriginal people seldom used it, as the plant's nutritional qualities are negligible.

IDENTIFICATION

Leaves and stalks (Fig. 1, i)

The diamond-shaped leaves have visible veins on their undersurface, and are covered with crystal-like drops 'sweating' from the leaves; they look as if they have been sprayed with water.

The main visual differences between the two forms of native spinach relate to the leaves and the branches. Bower spinach has smaller leaves than warrigals, reaching only 3–5 centimetres long, but its branches are longer than those of warrigals, growing up to 3 metres in length. Warrigal leaves can grow up to 15 centimetres, but the plant's branches only spread to a width of 1 metre.

Flowers and fruit (Fig. 1, ii)

The yellow flowers are hidden at the intersection between the branches and the leaves' stems. Warrigals produce pyramid-shaped fruits, 3–6 millimetres across; at first green, they mature to light brown to black, and are very tough. The fruits of bower spinach are 5–8 millimetres in diameter, round and berry-like; they mature to become light red and juicy.

AS FOOD

Native spinach is found on modern Australian menus as a topping on hipster pizzas, as a dumpling filling and as a boiled side green. The leaves are the only part of the plant eaten; they are harvested when young, as older leaves develop a pungent, acrid flavour.

In our house we mostly use this green as a replacement for common baby spinach. We blanch the leaves, and then mix them with other veggies and creamy sauces as a filler in pies and savoury vegetarian pastries.

Makes 8 flatbreads

Warrigal flatbread

INGREDIENTS

1½ cups steamed warrigal greens, cooled

3 garlic cloves

1½ tsp sea salt

2 tbsp extra virgin olive oil

¼ cup Greek-style yoghurt

2 cups wholemeal, plain or spelt flour

⅓ cup sparkling water

Extra flour for dusting

This is a perfect pairing with dandelion and macadamia pesto (p. 39).

1. Place the cooled warrigal greens, garlic, salt, olive oil and yoghurt in a blender. Process until smooth.

2. Place the flour in a medium-sized bowl and make a well in the centre. Add the warrigal paste and sparkling water. Using a wooden spoon, mix the paste into the flour to form a rough dough.

3. Dust a clean working surface with flour. Place the dough on the flour and knead it until smooth, then divide the dough into eight equal portions. Using your hands, form each portion into a round shape, flatten it with the palm of your hand and dust both sides with flour.

4. Use a rolling pin to roll each portion into a 15 cm round.

5. Heat a frying pan over medium heat. Fry the flatbreads for approximately 2–3 minutes on each side, until cooked and golden.

6. Place the cooked warrigal flatbreads in a tea towel and fold the edges over to cover and keep them warm.

7. Slice the flatbreads into wedges and serve with fresh pesto.

Cobbler's pegs

EDIBLE PARTS

leaf, flower

SNAPSHOT

Cobbler's pegs is a branched annual herb, growing up to 2 metres tall. It starts its growth cycle at any given opportunity, as long as there is adequate rainfall.

Bidens pilosa has a huge variety of common names (read the list below for the English language names alone), a testimony to how much attention it gets from humans all over the world. It's unlikely that you haven't noticed this plant before now. When I introduce it in my workshops, guests are a little puzzled at first, thrown by the scientific name – however, as soon as I show them a seed head and brush it against my socks, people recognise it right away. 'Oh, that one! I know that bloody thing! The seeds get stuck everywhere.'

That's right, you know it too. Walk through some overgrown, untidy patch of ground and you will find a bunch of fork-like seeds have stuck to your socks, your sleeves, your bag and even your dog's ears!

Cobbler's pegs is found all over the Australian continent, including the tropics.

Common names: beggar's tick, beggar-ticks, hairy beggar-ticks, black-jack, broom stick, broom stuff, cobbler's pegs, devil's needles, hairy bidens, Spanish needle, devil's pitchfork, farmer's friend and 'bloody thing'.

IDENTIFICATION

Leaves and stalks (Fig. 1, iii)

The leaves occur opposite one another on the stalks and are formed by three to seven leaflets (smaller leaves): one central, and the rest lateral and opposite. The leaflets can be up to 5 centimetres long, making the whole assemblage at times 20 centimetres long and 10 centimetres wide. The stalk is ribbed, sturdy and square in profile.

Flowers and seeds (Fig. 1, i, ii)

Cobbler's pegs produces flowers all year round. The flowers are small, 3–5 millimetres wide, with yellow heads that have four to five broad, white outer petals (ray florets). These showy petals drop as soon as the inner flower head has been pollinated, and that's when the seeds begin to develop. The seed heads form a ball of sticky 'ticks' that latch themselves onto clothes and animal fur.

Fig. 1 *Bidens pilosa*

AS FOOD

I have distilled this plant in gin, used it in salsa verde and pesto, added it to pasta sauces and stir-fries, and even featured it in a Vietnamese-style noodle salad. I love it. I grow it in my garden so that I do not need to go out to find it when I want it, and I use it regularly as a herb. The flavour is strong and complex. At first you taste resin and grass, but then it develops at the back of the palate with sage and oregano tones. It's an exciting flavour in my opinion.

AS MEDICINE

In traditional Chinese medicine, *Bidens pilosa* is called *xian feng cao* and is used for clearing heat (reducing stress and inflammation) and removing toxins. It is also extensively sourced by many traditional healers in Africa and Hawaii.

A friend of mine who is a herbalist and biologist loves this plant, and uses it regularly for its antibacterial properties, simply brewing a tea from the fresh or dried leaves and drinking it on a daily basis.

Fig. 2 Cobbler's pegs (*Bidens pilosa*) young shoot, flowers and seed heads.

Rumex species

Dock

EDIBLE PARTS

leaf, stalk, seed

SNAPSHOT

Dock is a perennial plant (it lives for many years underground) with a yearly cycle. This starts with new growth in spring, followed by the development of a flowering spike through the summer; the spike is made up of tiny, insignificant flowers, which soon form into green seeds. The whole plant can be up to 1.5 metres tall. The way to tell the various docks apart is by looking closely at the seeds – see the diagram on the following page for three examples – but if you mix up one with another, don't worry, all of them are edible, though not necessarily nice-tasting.

I remember as a young boy following my mum through the fields to do our seasonal jobs. We used to spend hours out in the sun, irrigating or cropping, harvesting or tending to the pastures. As young kids, my sisters and I would run around a lot, chasing insects and butterflies, poking sticks into little rodents' hollows or stalking frogs in the ditches. I distinctly remember at times whingeing about being hungry or thirsty – and my mum would turn her attention away from her task, look at me briefly, walk to the irrigation channels, pull up a leaf or two of *lavasoj* and state: 'We're nearly done, eat this, be quiet.' *Lavasoj* is the Piedmontese name for yellow dock (*Rumex crispus*). It was and still is a common weed in pastures in northern Italy, just as much as it is in the rest of the world.

I remember eating the stalk; the leaves were often too dry and bitter, but the stalk was juicy, tart and buttery. Then off I'd go, distracted again by a ladybug or grasshopper. I still eat dock: the young stalks from the leaves in the middle of the plant, where they are sticky with mucilage from the central growth. I harvest them straight from the fields and relive that flavour of butter and lemon from my childhood.

Rumex crispus (pictured opposite) grows in all Australian states and territories and is closely related to a number of other docks and sorrels in Australia, including native *Rumex brownii* (bilili in Wiradjuri or swamp dock in English), naturalised *Rumex obtusifolius* (broadleaved dock), and native *Rumex crystallinus* and *Rumex tenax* (both known as shiny dock). Probably the most famous of the genus would be *Rumex acetosa* (wild sorrel) and *Rumex acetosella* (sheep sorrel), exotic and now naturalised. You can find a relative of the dock plant anywhere in Australia.

i

ii

Fig. 1 *Rumex crispus*

Please note that dock contains medium levels of oxalic acid and should be blanched in boiling water for 10–15 seconds before consumption. (See wood sorrel, p. 58, for further information.)

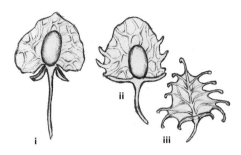

Fig. 2 Dock seeds comparison:
Rumex crispus (i), *Rumex obtusifolius* (ii)
and *Rumex brownii* (iii).

IDENTIFICATION

Leaves (Fig. 1, ii)

The leaves emerge from a central crown and range in form from a short stalk with a wide leaf to a long stalk with a narrower leaf. Alternate leaves also appear up the flowering spike as it grows. It is common to see the green leaves tainted with red dots and red edges due to damage by insects or parasites.

Flowers and seeds (Fig. 1, i; Fig. 2)

The flowering spike starts off green and turns purple-red at maturity. Seed clusters start off pea-green and then turn brown-red when they reach maturity. All dock seeds have three wings (known as valves) and are about 2–6 millimetres wide. Each species has differently shaped valves, some plain and some with hooks, but they always appear in sets of three.

Root

The root is a deep, carrot-like taproot, up to 1 metre long in healthy specimens.

AS FOOD

Humans have been eating dock since the beginning of our time on Earth, with archaeological evidence showing that dock seeds were part of the breakfast of an Iron Age man found in a peat bog in Denmark.

Nutritionally, the plant is well regarded for its high levels of iron and vitamins A and C, while the seeds of some species are used in gluten-free baked goods. The seeds can also be added to gruel or porridge, lending a tangy flavour to your breakfast.

The most commonly eaten part of the plant is its young leaves, harvested before the plant bolts up to flower. Not all docks are great to eat, as the flavour varies from colony to colony and can at times be very bitter. For this reason, do taste a little before using it. The dock that you want to make a soup with is either wild sorrel or sheep sorrel – both are excellent and tasty food, and much loved in French cuisine.

AS MEDICINE

The plant is used medicinally for the treatment of blood disorders like anaemia, and as a mild laxative in both Western herbalism and traditional Chinese medicine. In folk remedies it is used to relieve arthritis, purify the blood, aid liver function and treat skin conditions. Rubbing dock on the skin has long been regarded in Europe and the UK as an antidote to the pain caused by stinging nettles. Since both plants are common in wet areas, dock will usually be on hand. Modern herbal medicine doesn't prescribe this use, however; while dock *does* soothe the skin, there are usually better treatments for the pain of stinging nettle to be found nearby, such as plantain or chickweed.

Fig. 3 (opposite) Yellow dock (*Rumex crispus*)

Lactuca species

Wild lettuce

EDIBLE PARTS

leaf

SNAPSHOT

Wild lettuce is a biennial, fast-growing herb, reaching up to 2 metres in height. Any part of the plant will ooze a milky sap when cut.

Please note that the sap of wild lettuce contains lactucarium, which is a mild narcotic. Lactucarium levels increase towards the time of flowering.

Wild lettuce is regarded as the wild counterpart of the commercial lettuce you can buy at the supermarket. Although it is far more bitter than cultivated lettuce, it has greater nutritional and medicinal qualities. There are two varieties in Australia, found in all states and territories: wild lettuce (*Lactuca serriola*) – pictured opposite – and willowleaf lettuce (*Lactuca saligna*).

IDENTIFICATION

Leaves and stalks (Fig. 1, i)

The leaves at the base form a rosette and are larger (up to 25 centimetres long) than those growing up the flowering stalk. The leaves are oblong in shape and have prickles around the edges, as well as a distinctive line of prickles running up the spine on the underside of the leaf. The leaves of younger plants are wider and less indented, becoming deeply toothed as they grow older. The leaves of *Lactuca saligna* are substantially narrower than those of *Lactuca serriola*.

Flowers and seeds

The flowering stem is stiff, tall and hollow, and it can grow to 2 metres tall. In *Lactuca serriola*, it branches out at the top with up to twenty flowers. *Lactuca saligna* flowers are produced mainly on the stalk, with minimal branching at the very tip. The flowers are small and yellow, 10–15 millimetres wide, and develop a puff of seeds when fertilised.

AS FOOD

The best part of wild lettuce is the young leaves. I love the strong, bitter taste, but if you are not accustomed to this flavour I'd suggest eating the leaves combined with other less intensely flavoured greens. It is a renowned ingredient in Greek folk recipes like *hortapita* ('wild weeds' pie).

AS MEDICINE

The milky sap contains lactucarium, which has been used as medicine since antiquity for its digestive, diuretic, narcotic and sedative properties. Lactucarium is known as 'poor man's opium' and can be taken internally as an infusion for the treatment of anxiety, hyperactivity, insomnia, coughs, rheumatic pain and more.

I use this plant to make a tea for my wife when she's having trouble getting to sleep. It is mellow and effective. I always have some dry wild lettuce leaves in my dispensary, which I brew when needed. It is important *not* to boil the leaves, as very high heat will destroy the beneficial effects, so just place a few leaves in a teapot, add hot (but not boiling) water and let it infuse for a few minutes.

Fig. 1 *Lactuca serriola*

Urtica species

Nettle

EDIBLE PARTS

leaf, seed, shoot

SNAPSHOT

Nettle is an erect, branched perennial plant with a yearly cycle. It dies off after seeding to sprout back up with new growth when conditions are right.

Please note that nettle is covered in stinging hairs that cause painful skin irritation. Always wear gloves when engaging with this plant.

Nettle is amazing. Super nutritious, it improves your health and the health of the soil where it grows (and is an incredible source of very strong weaving fibre!). But if it rubs against your skin, it hurts, so be mindful when interacting with nettle.

Put simply, the reason that nettle hurts is because it has hollow, prickly little 'hairs' all over it; when these pierce the skin, a bulb at the base releases pain-causing chemicals. If you touch any part of the plant, it will sting you and – depending on the species – will irritate your skin for up to two days.

I was stung *so* many times by this plant in my youth, when I was working in the fields during summer. I would absentmindedly brush my leg against it, and within three to five seconds the itchiness of the sting would begin, quickly developing into a searing irritation that could persist for hours! It definitely kept me awake and alert while I was working.

When engaging with this plant, wear gloves. You can ensure there's no chance of being stung by rubbing the hairs from the nettle with your gloved hands, or by drying, boiling or grilling the harvested plant.

There are three varieties of nettles in Australia.

Giant nettle (*Urtica dioica*)

This exotic is naturalised in Australia, but is not very common. It grows to a height of 150 centimetres and has oval- or diamond-shaped leaves up to 10 centimetres long.

Small nettle (*Urtica urens*)

This exotic species (pictured opposite) is naturalised all over Australia. Small nettle grows to a height of 60 centimetres. Its leaves are smaller than those of the giant nettle, up to 6 centimetres long.

Native nettle (*Urtica incisa*)

Found all over south-eastern Australia, this native species grows up to 1 metre tall. Its leaves grow to a length of 10 centimetres and are distinctly narrower than those of the other species.

Fig. 1 *Urtica dioica*

Fig. 2 Small nettle (*Urtica urens*)

IDENTIFICATION

Flowers and seeds (Fig. 1, i)

In all species, the flowers are small (only 1–3 millimetres across), white to cream in colour, and grow in short clusters that arise where the leaves emerge from the stalk. The flower clusters are 1–3 centimetres long in *Urtica urens* and *Urtica dioica*, and considerably longer (up to 5 centimetres) in *Urtica incisa*. The seeds mature in late summer.

AS FOOD

Nettle is a very valuable addition to the diet, a highly nutritious food that is easily digested and high in minerals (especially iron) and vitamins (especially A and C). Cooking the leaves, or thoroughly drying them, neutralises the stinging potential of the hairs and their chemicals, rendering the leaf safe to eat. Nettle beer is brewed from the young shoots, while nettle seeds are regarded as a super food. An Aboriginal friend of mine taught me a great camping hack with nettle. You collect the plant, stalk and all (use gloves or a rolled-up shirt), and place the branches on stones near a fire. They will cook in the heat, neutralising the sting and turning into excellent nettle chips. All you need is nettle, fire and salt.

Read on for a recipe that I developed with plant-based chef Joey Astorga for an event in country New South Wales – feeding stinging nettles to farmers. It was a hit!

AS MEDICINE

Nettle has a long history of use as a folk remedy and is commonly prescribed as a herbal supplement by naturopaths across the globe. A tea made from the leaves has traditionally been used as a tonic and blood purifier.

Historically, the fresh plant has been used to treat arthritic pain, with the stinging leaves being rubbed onto the affected areas to activate blood flow. Applying a decoction of nettle as a hair tonic is a renowned folk remedy for the treatment of dandruff.

Stinging nettle focaccia

INGREDIENTS

8 cups fresh nettle leaves

2 tsp (1 × 7 g sachet) dried yeast

2 tsp caster sugar

3 cups plain flour

Olive oil for greasing the baking tin and brushing the focaccia

2 tbsp fresh rosemary leaves

2 tsp sea salt flakes

1. Blanch the nettle leaves in salty boiling water. Drain, then rinse in cold water. Remove any stalks, chop the leaves roughly and set aside.

2. Mix all the dry ingredients together in a large bowl. Make a well in the centre, then slowly incorporate 1¼ cups of warm water and work this into a dough.

3. Turn the dough out onto a floured surface and knead gently for 5 minutes.

4. Put the dough in a bowl that has been coated with a little olive oil. Cover with a clean tea towel and leave to rise for about 1 hour in a warm place (around 30 °C is ideal, so on top of your warm oven is a good spot).

5. Knead back the risen dough, then add the blanched nettle and the rosemary. Keep kneading to fully incorporate the nettle. Let the dough rest for another hour.

6. Oil a rectangular, shallow baking tin (I use a 25 × 35 cm tin). Tip the dough onto the work surface, then stretch it to fill the tin. Cover with a tea towel and allow to rest for another 30 minutes. Preheat your oven to 200 °C fan-forced or 220 °C conventional.

7. Bake for 10 minutes, then lower the temperature to 160 °C fan-forced/180 °C conventional and bake for another 5 minutes.

8. Remove the focaccia from the oven and leave it to cool for 5 minutes in its baking tin. Brush with a generous amount of olive oil, lightly sprinkle with sea salt, then remove from the tin and transfer to a wire cooling rack.

9. Serve with olive oil for dipping, or with your favourite spread, and enjoy.

Brassica species

Wild brassicas

EDIBLE PARTS

leaf, flower

SNAPSHOT

Wild brassicas are annual or biennial plants, bright emerald-green to dark olive in colour. Usually growing to half a metre tall, they sometimes reach 1.5 metres when in full flower.

Wild brassica is a common name for a number of related species, all edible, all introduced and naturalised, all with a similar flavour profile. Many of the *Brassica* species are now interbreeding, creating various hybrids and localised colonies.

The easiest way to approach this group of plants is by empowering yourself with knowledge of the typical identification features. Once you've confirmed a plant is one of the wild brassicas, try it for yourself, as the taste varies from a spicy mustard to bland cabbage flavour. The most common weed species of the brassica family in south-eastern Australia are wild turnip (*Brassica tournefortii*), field mustard (*Brassica rapa*), wild cabbage (*Brassica oleracea*), brown mustard (*Brassica juncea*) and rapeseed (*Brassica napus*). Many of these wild weeds have been domesticated over the centuries and are now common vegetables, making the distinction between weed and useful plant quite blurry.

Don't feel overwhelmed – you just need to familiarise yourself with some key features and then off you go, free veggies forever!

IDENTIFICATION

Leaves (Fig. 1, ii)

Wild brassicas have variable leaves, smooth when young but developing bristle-like hairs when older. The lower leaves can be quite wide and up to 30 centimetres long, while the leaves developing up the flowering stalks are noticeably smaller.

Flowers and seeds (Fig. 1, i)

The flowers are the distinguishing feature, as they have a cross-like shape, formed by four petals – usually yellow, but sometimes white – with a central cluster of four tall and two short stamens (stamens being the male part of the flower). They range from a few millimetres wide to 25–30 millimetres, depending on species and conditions. If you see a yellow-flowered, low-lying weed, come closer – if the flowers have the distinctive cross shape, chances are this is a brassica. The seeds are formed in elongated seed pods that resemble tiny beans pointing upwards; brassica seed pods can be differentiated from those of the bean family (*Fabaceae*) by their two internal chambers, which have seeds distributed between them.

Fig. 1 *Brassica* species

AS FOOD

All wild brassicas are edible, but they vary greatly in flavour, depending on where they grow or the traits of the particular colony. At times they can be quite bitter.

Another important aspect to consider is texture. While the very young leaves are usually good as a raw addition to salads, the older leaves quickly become fibrous and hairy, and are best enjoyed cooked or fermented. In my opinion the most delicious and easiest-to-use part of the plant is the flowers, always abundant throughout most of the year. They are fresh and juicy, and distinctively cabbage-flavoured, but nevertheless pleasant as a snack when out in the fields (or used as a garnish for a dish).

Brassicas are a highly respected vegetable, providing nutritious amounts of vitamin C, vitamin K, magnesium and soluble fibre.

Fig. 2 Wild brassica (*Brassica* species) in flower.

Typha species

Bulrush

EDIBLE PARTS

flower, pollen, root, shoot

SNAPSHOT

Bulrush is a perennial water plant with a yearly cycle. Wherever it grows, it forms an extensive network of underground (and underwater) rhizomes. The plant produces new shoots in springtime that can grow to a height of 2 metres.

There are some plants that are so ingrained in our visual vocabulary that they have become symbols. This is the case for bulrushes. If you think of a pond or marshlands, you visualise bulrushes with their tall stalks and cigar-shaped brown flowering spikes.

We humans have been eating and using bulrushes forever, all over the world. In Italy, we still use it for weaving chair seats and to protect glass bottles of wine – the typical Chianti wine look. Bulrush is found across Australia, from the tropics to the desert, and has traditionally been a staple part of the diet of Aboriginal and Torres Strait Islander people.

There are three types of bulrush in Australia: the native narrow-leaved cumbungi (*Typha domingensis*) – pictured opposite – widespread throughout the continent; the native broadleaved cumbungi (*Typha orientalis*), mostly coastal; and the exotic bulrush (*Typha latifolia*), less widespread, mostly confined to south-eastern Victoria and Tasmania.

IDENTIFICATION

Leaves and stalks (Fig. 1, i)

The leaves are bluish-green and narrow, extending upwards from the rhizome nodes and growing up to 1 metre in length and 50–80 millimetres wide. The long, straight stems are round in cross-section and can grow to 3 metres tall.

Flowers and seeds

The flowers are the main feature of this self-pollinating plant, and the most recognisable part. At the end of each flower spike there are two sets of swollen 'cobs', packed with tiny flowers – the male cob at the top and the female below it. The male cob will disappear after pollinating the female flowers, while the female cob, which is green at first, will develop seeds and turn brown once it has been fertilised. These brown seeds soon form a kind of fluff, which is picked up by the wind or drops to the water below; the seeds then germinate in mud or in water, forming rhizomes.

Root (Fig. 1, ii)

The roots form an underground network of rhizomes and spread and establish themselves by colonising the surrounding area. The rhizomes form nodes; from these, new shoots will rise up as reeds. When you harvest the new shoots they will be quite crunchy, while later in life they become very fibrous and stringy.

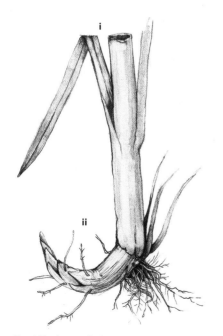

Fig. 1 *Typha* species

Fig. 2 (opposite) Narrow-leaved cumbungi (*Typha domingensis*)

AS FOOD

The most commonly eaten parts of the plant are the young shoots and the flowering cobs when green. They can be roasted, eaten raw or added to soups.

The young shoots taste similar to sweet corn, and a very nutritious flour can be extracted from the stalks and roots by drying them and bashing the starch out of the fibrous parts.

Another interesting product sourced from this plant is the pollen, which can be collected from the male flowering spikes and used in baking as a protein-rich additive for flour. It has a mild, sweet taste, starchy but very pleasant when fresh.

I like to eat the stalks of young plants, straight from the pond, with my feet wet. I pull up the stalk, peel it back to the inner, crunchy, juicy parts, and enjoy it there and then. It really tastes like sweet corn.

Below I share another recipe developed with chef Joey Astorga for an event. I have made this several times since, and the trick to it is freshness: you really need to find fresh shoots and use them within a day. The result is a crisp, surprising and filling salad.

Serves 6

Cumbungi and sow thistle slaw

INGREDIENTS

1 garlic clove, crushed

½ small red onion, finely sliced

1 tsp Dijon mustard

1 cup whole egg mayonnaise

1 tbsp apple cider vinegar

1 bunch dill, chopped

1 bunch parsley leaves, chopped

¼ purple cabbage, shredded

15–20 young cumbungi or bulrush shoots, finely sliced (*you will need to peel off the outer layers of the cumbungi stalks to get down to the young shoots inside, which are the sweet, crunchy part you want for this recipe*)

4 cups sow thistle leaves, finely chopped

Salt and pepper to taste

Optional: add grated carrot or finely sliced red capsicum for more colour

1. Mix together the garlic, onion, mustard, mayonnaise, vinegar and herbs to make a dressing.

2. Toss the cabbage, bulrush shoots and sow thistle together in a large bowl.

3. Season the dressing with salt and pepper, mix through the salad and serve.

4. Share your harvesting tale to impress your dinner guests.

Galium aparine

Cleavers

EDIBLE PARTS

seed, shoot

SNAPSHOT

Cleavers is a bright-green annual rambler that climbs over other plants, forming sprawling mats, 1 to several metres wide.

The story goes that this is the plant that sparked the idea for Velcro strips! Engineered by nature with the ability to 'hook' onto any surface, cleavers or 'sticky weed' can be found from Brisbane to Adelaide, and even in the region around Perth.

IDENTIFICATION

Leaves and stalks (Fig. 1, i)

The leaves sprout in clusters of six to eight, forming a circle around the nodes. They are lance-like in shape, 20–80 millimetres long and up to 10 millimetres wide. The stalks are angular, usually square in profile, very fragile and branched, and 2–4 millimetres thick. The whole plant is covered with tiny hooks that cling to your clothes as you brush past them.

Flowers and seeds (Fig. 1, ii)

The flowers are 1–2 millimetres wide and white in colour. They develop into bristly seed pods, which are 3–6 millimetres across and divided into two chambers. The seeds are round and rough, about 2–3 millimetres in size.

AS FOOD

This plant is very beneficial, yet quite hard to eat, as it is stringy, bitter and bristly. The best part of the plant is the seeds, which can be collected rather quickly – and in quantity – by using a cloth, as the seeds will stick to the fabric. The seeds need only a little drying before being lightly roasted; although they taste very similar to coffee, they have the healthy properties of a tonic as opposed to being a stimulant. A decoction using the whole dried plant results in a drink similar to black tea.

Young shoots are good too, if cooked in soups or added to casseroles.

AS MEDICINE

Cleavers has a long history of domestic medicinal use and is widely prescribed by modern herbalists. As an ingredient for medicines, the plant is harvested as it comes into flower, and can be used fresh or dried. It is administered both internally and externally in the treatment of a wide range of ailments: for example, as a poultice for wounds, ulcers and many other skin problems; as a decoction for insomnia; and in cases where a strong diuretic is beneficial. The plant is often used as part of a spring tonic drink, along with other herbs like chickweed and dandelion.

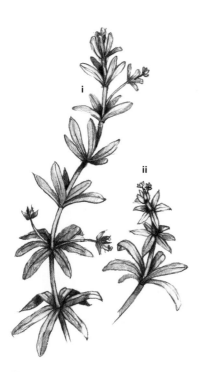

Fig. 1 *Galium aparine*

Chapter 05

✳   This chapter focuses on migrant cultural knowledge as a lived experience. It reveals the foraging narratives of Australia's Eastern European and Mediterranean migrants and reflects on what it means to find connections.

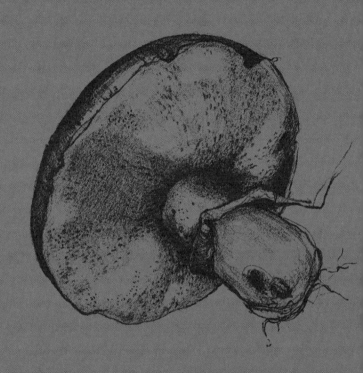

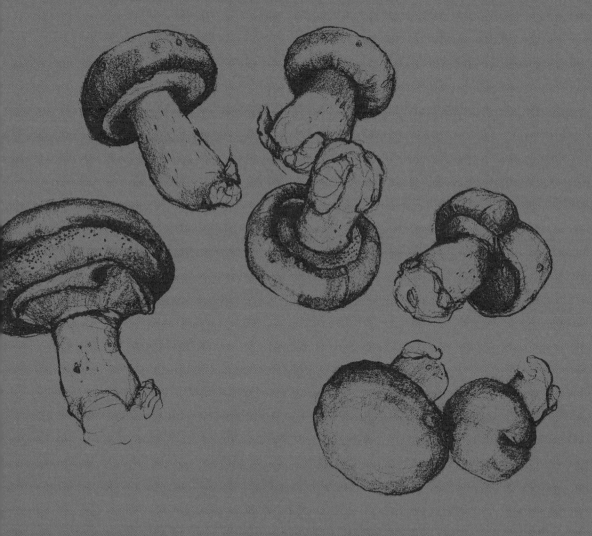

Forest

Forest

The light streams through the pine trees, smoke-like with the early morning mist and our warm breath. All around us, the smell of damp dirt and pine cones. This is a truly magical place. It is quiet and welcoming, the soft needles muffling our steps as we discover the wonders and peculiarities of this powerful ecosystem.

State forests in Australia are often planted with hectares of plantation pines. When the summer is gone and the days become shorter, wetter and colder, the forests are the site of one of the most exhilarating adventures and communions with nature: wild pine mushroom foraging.

What we term 'pine mushrooms' - the edible seasonal treat that people harvest from pine plantations on the east coast of Australia - come with a tale that has migrant origins; more specifically, Polish, Italian, Russian and Eastern European roots.

The story goes that at some point earlier last century, the spores of edible mushrooms made it to the pine forests of Australia. Some say the forests were deliberately inoculated, others say the fungi came attached to the roots of early tree imports. It's even been said that forestry corporations (the managers of pine plantations in Australia) introduced the mycelia of a number of beneficial mushrooms to enable the trees to thrive and grow faster. Whatever the story, the migrant community of Australia knew straight away what these introduced mushrooms were and what to do with. Eat them!

Fast-forward to now. This cultural practice, closely guarded for generations, suddenly explodes into seasonal edible adventures, an alternative economy for regional people and a culinary treat on the tables of some of the fanciest restaurants in the country.

It is not unusual for second and third generation Italian or Polish Australian people to spend their youth in state forests with their extended families, celebrating the deep-seated heritage that is mushroom foraging. Learning language and recipes, connecting with family and place, celebrating culture and ties to cultural knowledge. Fostering a sense of belonging and legitimacy in a foreign country, speaking a foreign language among a forest of exotic trees. Anyone who has lived far from home will know the comfort of finding a familiar landscape or experience that evokes a reference to one's homeland and acts as a cultural grounding point.

What is a mushroom?

Fungi are not plants, nor are they animals – they are a separate kingdom. A mushroom is the reproductive strategy of an organism – mycelium – that lives underground. All fungi have a mycelium, but not all mycelia produce mushrooms.

Some mushrooms have gills, some have pores, some are like jellies and others are like puffballs, but all of them produce spores to reproduce. Spores are essentially a micro version of the fungi, and when a spore lands in favourable conditions, it joins with other spores and starts the process of creating a mycelium.

Most fungi have established evolutionary partnerships with other kingdoms – sometimes with animals, but mostly with plants and algae. They need this relationship in order to thrive. Some relationships are mutually beneficial, while others are exploitative. The mushrooms that I discuss in this chapter have mutual relationships with pines.

To identify mushrooms correctly, you need to be aware of some key identification features:

Habitat: where the mushroom grows, and nearby vegetation

Substrate: what the mushroom grows on

Habit: whether the mushroom grows in clusters, alone or in colonies

Cap (also known as the pileus): shape, colour and texture

Gills (also known as lamellae): whether the mushroom has gills or pores, or neither; if present, their colour and shape, and how they attach to the stalk

Stalk (also known as the stipe): size, colour and shape

Skirt (also known as the annulus): presence, shape and colour

Volva: whether the mushroom grows out of an 'egg' or not

Fig. 1 Mushroom features

i Warts; **ii** Cap (pileus); **iii** Scales; **iv** Skin (cuticle); **v** Pores;
vi Skirt (annulus); **vii** Stalk (stipe); **viii** Mycelium; **ix** Egg sack (volva);
x Markings; **xi** Spores; **xii** Gills (lamellae)

Picking the known

There are an estimated 7000 to 8000 mushroom-producing fungi species in Australia, the vast majority of which have yet to be described. So, when out in the forest, we are just going to pick the known ones, the ones we are confident we can eat, those that have been catalogued and tested and eaten by generations of foragers.

That is why, when I run wild edible mushroom workshops, I only ever teach three species: saffron milk caps, slippery Jacks and slippery Jills. Yes, there are other known edible mushrooms out there – like the wood blewits, grey knights and the elusive porcini – but many of these are rare, and require a depth of knowledge beyond the scope of novice wildcrafters. If you are new to mushrooming, you stick to the basics.

If you've never foraged for mushrooms before, it is important to find an experienced harvester to show you around. There is nothing like firsthand experience when learning the difference between mushroom species. A knowledgeable guide will make you aware of the dos and don'ts, equipping you with a valuable life skill: harvesting your own food. Imagine that. Fresh mushrooms every year from your local forest!

Once you empower yourself with the knowledge of the key features of these edibles, you won't make mistakes – and that's where you want to be.

An important note on identifying mushrooms

There is only one way to know if what you are looking at is the mushroom that you think it is, and that is by systematically going through ALL of the identification features and ticking each box. If even just one of the features is dubious, you leave the mushroom alone. 'Kind-of' or 'close-enough' assessments are a sure way to make mistakes. You HAVE to be pedantic. Sometimes there are variables – some mushrooms are slightly different, odd, not textbook examples of their kind – but until you are perfectly confident in your mushrooming skills and highly experienced with the species, you leave the odd ones alone, or get them checked by someone who knows.

Forest legalities and ethics

Pine mushrooms are not free food, they are a gift. Please treat them as such. Respect the forest as the precious ecosystem that it is, whether it is a plantation or not. Take your rubbish out with you, and stick to tracks and roads when walking or driving through the forest. When you look after these amazing ecosystems, you will be richly rewarded. A happy pine forest is a generous one. Only ever pick what you will use that day or preserve that night.

Foraging for mushrooms is possible and legal anywhere on private land. As for public land, the rules vary from state to state. In New South Wales, foraging for pine mushrooms in state forests is allowed and a recognised activity. In Victoria, pine plantations are managed privately, and foraging is tolerated as long as you have secured access permission (an online form). In South Australia, Tasmania and Western Australia, the foraging situation is more complex, and I exhort you to seek out information from your local organisation.

A young slippery Jack
(*Suillus luteus*).

'I've been a regular visitor to Belanglo since 1986, when at the age of nine I migrated to Australia from Poland ... We went there because the pine forest and its surrounds resembled Poland - the "homeland" - perhaps more than any other part of Australia we knew; but most of all we went there for the mushrooms, three edible varieties of which sprouted among pine needles on the forest floor. And we were not alone. Mushroom hunting in pine plantations was quite a popular pastime among the Polish community of Sydney and over the years Belanglo had developed into a significant destination. Each year would see more and more parked cars and mushroom hunters scattered throughout the woods ... Belanglo had effectively become a Polish space - an outpost of Poland, or more specifically the Polish community of Sydney, in a corner of the Southern Highlands that for many years did not even register as a blip on the radar screens of most Australians, even locals.'

— Dr Max Kwiatkowski, author of 'Re-creating the Polish "homelandscape":
Mushroom hunting in Belanglo' from *Polonia in Australia*

Lactarius deliciosus

Saffron milk cap

EDIBLE PARTS

cap, stalk

SNAPSHOT

You are looking for a bright carrot-orange mushroom, irregular in shape and with distinctive marks on the cap and stalk. Key to the species is the bright orange 'milk' (latex) that exudes from any part of the mushroom when it is cut or broken. Saffron milk caps only last a few days in the forest: by the time the mushroom is a week old, it will be either dry and woody, or mushy and discoloured. Either way, the latex – key to identification – will not be present. Only ever harvest good specimens.

The whole mushroom is speckled with reddish-orange markings and pitted as if it has been bombarded by meteors.

The saffron milk cap is found under pine trees across south-eastern Australia, from south of Brisbane to Tasmania and South Australia. They have never been recorded in Western Australia. You will find them under older trees where the pine needles are thicker. Depending on conditions (temperature and rain), they are in season from March to June.

IDENTIFICATION

Cap (Fig. 1, i)

This starts off shaped like a button and grows into a trumpet-like cap. The mature shape is highly variable and irregular, with a dip in the centre. The mushroom grows to dinner-plate size in favourable conditions. Concentric circles are visible on the top of the cap, created by lighter and darker shades of orange.

Underside (Fig. 1, ii)

Saffron milk caps are part of the agarics group, hence they have gills on the underside of the cap. The gills are attached to the stalk and radiate out. They are a consistent orange in colour, but are easily bruised, turning green-blue when this occurs.

Spores

The spores are cream in colour.

Stalk (Fig. 1, iii)

The stalk is stout, hollow and about 2–5 centimetres long by 2–5 centimetres wide. It tapers to a small point at the base.

Flesh

The flesh is brittle, white-cream in colour in the stalk and carrot-orange in the cap, with distinctive bright-orange milk oozing out when the mushroom is damaged.

Location

Found under pine trees across south-eastern Australia. This species is symbiotic with *Pinus* species (pine trees). If you are not under a pine tree you are not looking at a saffron milk cap.

AS FOOD

Saffron milk caps are flavoursome and slightly peppery; generally speaking, they are quite firm, meaty mushrooms. A classic recipe involves frying the sliced mushrooms in a pan with oil and a little garlic, then serving hot with a sprinkle of parsley. They are also delicious cooked in a risotto – I give a recipe for risotto made with pine mushrooms and sorrel on page 201.

Fig. 1 *Lactarius deliciosus*

Fig. 2 Saffron milk cap (*Lactarius deliciosus*): note the orange milk oozing out of this fresh specimen.

Pine mushroom and sorrel risotto

INGREDIENTS

1 tbsp olive oil

1 brown onion, finely chopped

2 cups sliced fresh or pickled pine mushrooms
(*see pickling recipe on p. 207*)

1 garlic clove, crushed

1½ cups arborio rice

1 cup dry white wine

1 L vegetable or chicken-style liquid stock

1 cup fresh sorrel leaves, to serve

Shaved parmesan cheese, to serve (*leave out
for vegan*)

1. Heat the oil in a large, heavy-based saucepan over medium–high heat. Add the brown onion and pine mushrooms. Cook, stirring, for 5 minutes or until softened.

2. Add the garlic and rice. Cook, stirring, for 1 minute, then add the wine.

3. Bring the mixture to the boil. Cook, stirring, for 3 minutes or until the liquid has almost evaporated. Reduce the heat to low.

4. Add one ladleful of stock to the rice. Cook, stirring, until the rice has absorbed the liquid. Repeat with the remaining stock mixture, one ladleful at a time.

5. Serve the risotto with the fresh sorrel, and shaved parmesan if desired.

Suillus luteus

Slippery Jack

EDIBLE PARTS

cap, stalk – remove skin and underside

SNAPSHOT

The *Suillus* mushrooms are part of the Boletales order (like the porcini), and unlike the saffron milk cap, they have pores on the underside. These pores are essentially small tubular holes that produce and expel the spores when the mushroom is mature. When you look at the underside, it has the appearance of a fine sponge. The main difference between the slippery Jack and slippery Jill is that the slippery Jack has a 'skirt', or ring around the stalk, while the slippery Jill does not. You are looking out for a slimy mushroom growing under pine needles, with a sponge-like underside that is off-white turning lime-yellow.

Please note that it is best to peel the skin and the underside from these mushrooms before eating, as they can be heavy to digest.

There are two common varieties of *Suillus* mushrooms in the pine forest: slippery Jack and slippery Jill. They are very similar: both are edible and both grow in the same conditions at the same time, found in pine plantations across south-eastern and south-western Australia. Depending on conditions, they are in season from April to June. It is common to find slippery Jacks (and slippery Jills) in groups, growing one on top of the other. The older ones (three to seven days old) tend to become infested with slugs.

IDENTIFICATION

Cap (Fig. 1, i)

Brown in colour and up to 20 centimetres in diameter at maturity, the cap is initially globe-like, later flattening out. It is slimy to the touch, smooth and glossy even when dry. The skin (cuticle) is easily peeled off.

Underside (Fig. 1, ii)

Rather than gills, the spongy underside features tiny, circular pores; initially a light yellow in colour, they turn dark yellow to olive green with maturity.

Spores

The spores are clay to ochre in colour.

Stalk (Fig. 1, iii)

The stalk is white to cream in colour, stout, rather short at 2.5–5 centimetres long, and features a large veil/ring. In young specimens, the veil is white and attached to the cap. It then darkens to purple-brown and detaches from the cap to form a ring, which in turn disappears in older specimens, leaving purple marks on the stalk.

Flesh

The flesh is pale yellow or white, and silky in texture.

Location

Found in pine plantations across south-eastern and south-western Australia, under older trees where the pine needles are thicker.

AS FOOD

See the information for slippery Jill on the following page.

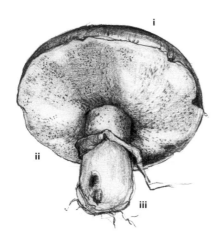

Fig. 1 *Suillus luteus*

Slippery Jill

EDIBLE PARTS

cap, stalk – remove skin and underside

SNAPSHOT

You are looking out for a slimy mushroom growing under pine needles, with a whitish, sponge-like underside. Unlike the very similar slippery Jack, the stalk of the slippery Jill features distinctive 'grainy' marks and does not have a 'skirt'.

The cap is slimy, unless conditions have been very dry. It is common to see bite marks from slugs, particularly on the underside, as well as tiny torn areas.

Growing in the same conditions and at the same time as the slippery Jack, the slippery Jill is found in pine plantations across south-eastern and south-western Australia. Depending on conditions, it is in season from April to June.

IDENTIFICATION

Cap (Fig. 1, i)

Light brown and up to 12 centimetres in diameter at maturity, the cap is initially globe-like, later flattening out. It is slimy to the touch, smooth and glossy even when dry. The skin is easily peeled off.

Underside (Fig. 1, iii)

Rather than gills, the spongy underside features tiny, circular pores; initially a light yellow in colour, they turn dark yellow to olive green with maturity. It is common to see tiny droplets being exuded from the underside of young specimens.

Spores

The spores are ochre or sienna-brown in colour.

Stalk (Fig. 1, ii)

White to cream in colour, cylindrical in shape, and rather short at 2.5–5 centimetres long, the stalk has distinctive marks that make it look 'grainy' (hence the species name *granulatus*).

Flesh

The flesh is pale yellow or white in colour.

Location

Found in pine plantations across south-eastern and south-western Australia, under older trees where the pine needles are thicker.

AS FOOD

There are so many recipes for pine mushrooms, from mushroom schnitzel, soups and dips, to mushroom pies.

There are also several ways to preserve this seasonal bounty. You can fry them in a pan and then freeze in small parcels. You can make a soup, reduce it until it is quite thick and then freeze it. You can either air-dry pine mushrooms or dry them in a dehydrator. My favourite way to preserve them is by pickling. I grew up on a similar recipe to the one I've shared on page 207. This pickling recipe should only serve as a guide – experiment until you find the recipe you like best.

Fig. 1 *Suillus granulatus*

Fig. 2 Top to bottom: slippery Jill (*Suillus granulatus*) and slippery Jack (*Suillus luteus*) cap and stalk.

Fig. 3 Top to bottom: slippery Jill (*Suillus granulatus*) and slippery Jack (*Suillus luteus*) underside.

Pickled pine mushrooms

INGREDIENTS

500 g pine mushrooms

500 ml white wine vinegar

4 garlic cloves

4 sprigs rosemary

300 ml olive oil

1. Slice the mushrooms. Slippery Jacks and Jills will also need to be peeled.

2. In a large saucepan, add the vinegar to 1 L of water and bring to the boil.

3. Add the mushrooms and simmer for approximately 10 minutes, or until soft.

4. Sterilise two 250 ml pickling jars (see p. 52). Once cooled, add two cloves of garlic and a sprig of rosemary to each jar.

5. Strain the vinegar water from the cooked mushrooms. Spoon equal amounts of the still-hot mushrooms into the two jars and cover generously with the oil, making sure the mushrooms are completely submerged. I like to use an extra sprig of rosemary jammed in sideways to help keep the mushrooms under the oil.

6. Seal and label the jars, including the date made. To check that your jars are well sealed, while they are still warm turn them upside down for a few minutes.

7. Store in a cool, dark and dry place for up to a year. Refrigerate once opened and use within 3 months.

Mushrooms for the experienced forager

The following mushrooms are a teaser. I present them just as a point of interest, and they should only be seen as proof that there is so much more out there. We are barely scratching the surface of the possibilities of fungi, and the three species discussed on the following pages are found in the same forests where you would find the saffron milk cap and the slippery Jack/Jill. The following mushrooms are for more experienced people, though, and should only be approached with caution, *after* you have walked with an expert forager who can show you how to properly identify and process them.

It is worth noting that the vast majority of knowledge about edible mushrooms is in relation to exotic species. Little knowledge is left of traditional usage of fungi by Aboriginal people, due to the process of colonisation and systemic degradation of culture. It is my hope that with the offering of exotic knowledge in relation to species that live in Australia today, we can rekindle the magic of connection, care and understanding – even in an area as mysterious as the fungi kingdom.

Tricholoma terreum

Grey knight

EDIBLE PARTS

cap

SNAPSHOT

The best way to explain the appearance of grey knights is to say that the cap looks like the back of a mouse: furry, and grey to grey-brown in colour, with bright white gills underneath.

The grey knight is found in pine plantations across south-eastern and south-western Australia, under older trees where the pine needles are thicker. Depending on conditions, it is in season from April to June. Grey knights appear in clusters or alone and are far less common than the saffron milk cap or the slippery Jack/Jill.

IDENTIFICATION

Cap (Fig. 1, i)

The cap is 4–7 centimetres across. It is grey to light brown and evenly covered in fine, silky scales that reflect the light, giving it a fur-like appearance. The cap is convex, with a slight indent on one side, and broadly conical in shape.

Underside (Fig. 1, ii)

The grey knight is a gilled mushroom. The lamellae are white, with a tinge of yellowing in older specimens (three to five days old), although the change is quite slow and subtle. The gills are wide apart and not attached to the stalk.

Spores

The spores are white in colour.

Stalk (Fig. 1, iii)

The stalk is off-white, visibly fibrous when you break it, and about 3–8 centimetres long and 1.5 centimetres wide. It is cylindrical and has no ring around it.

Flesh

The flesh is white to off-white, and easily damaged. It has a pleasant mild hazelnut smell.

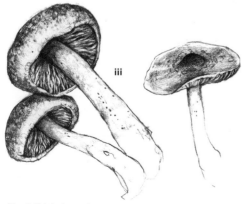

Fig. 1 *Tricholoma terreum*

211

Amanita muscaria

Fly agaric

SNAPSHOT

This is the classic fairytale mushroom: red cap with white dots. When you see it, you'll know. This mushroom emerges from the ground covered in a white, capsule-like, protective sac (volva) – it looks a lot like an egg.

It will grow quickly and tall, making it a great lamp-post in the forest, visible from afar – heralding the start of the mushroom season.

Please note that fly agaric is toxic unless properly processed.

Fly agaric is regarded as toxic, although records of deaths from ingesting this toadstool are extremely rare. Some cultural groups in Russia, Japan and North America regularly ingest this mushroom after boiling it and leaching out the toxins. It has also been used in shamanic practices because of its hallucinogenic components, which are active when fly agaric is eaten raw.

Fly agaric is found in association with a wide variety of conifers and deciduous trees. It has been recorded from southern Queensland, through New South Wales and Tasmania, to South Australia and Western Australia. Depending on conditions (temperature and rain), it is in season from March to June.

IDENTIFICATION

Cap (Fig. 1, i)

The cap is 8–20 centimetres in diameter and evenly covered in fine white dots when young: the remnants of the egg sac it came out of. These dots will spread out as the cap expands, and might wash off in heavy rain. The cap changes from a ball to a half-spherical shape, before flattening out at maturity. It is likely that it will lose some of its colour at maturity, turning from bright red to orange to a dull yellow.

Underside (Fig. 1, ii)

Fly agaric has white gills, unchanging with maturity. The gills are free (not attached to the stalk).

Spores

The spores are white in colour.

Stalk (Fig. 1, iii)

Off-white, 5–20 centimetres long and 1–2 centimetres wide, the stalk is slightly conical, wider at the base where it emerges from the 'egg'. There are visible remnants of rings around the base of the stalk. The stalk's surface can appear flaky and the consistency is noticeably fibrous.

Flesh

The flesh is white to off-white, easily damaged and with no particular smell, except for a slight 'earthiness'.

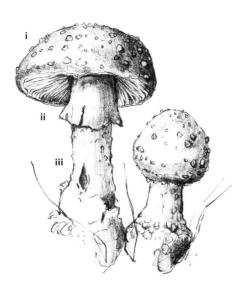

Fig. 1 *Amanita muscaria*

Fig. 2 Fly agaric (*Amanita muscaria*) cap.

Fig. 3 Fly agaric (*Amanita muscaria*) growth habit.

Boletus edulis

Porcini

EDIBLE PARTS

cap, stalk

SNAPSHOT

This is the kind of mushroom that gets people hunting for years on end, scouting locations and slowly accumulating knowledge from fellow foragers. I never knew anyone who 'bumped into' a porcini. Rather, when you *do* find it, it is the kind of mushroom that represents the completion of a process of stalking. It is the moment the rewards come in.

When you see people boasting online about finding their porcini and it was all too easy, it is invariably one of the woody, native *Boletus*: not edible – and quite disappointing, when your porcini-hunting bubble bursts. But when you find the real one, it is all worth it. In Australia, it is only found in the Adelaide Hills and some forests in Victoria. I have been told that people have found some in New South Wales too, but no one would tell me where exactly. Secret porcini business. Totally worth it.

This well-loved mushroom is a little tease. We do indeed have the amazing and much-celebrated porcini growing in Australia, but in reality it is only found in the Adelaide Hills. It is believed that *Boletus edulis* was accidentally introduced in the 1800s, when colonists imported trees from Europe. DNA testing has confirmed that this occasionally abundant seasonal treat is identical to the porcini of Europe. So, if you ever want to set aside some time for mushroom tourism, South Australia is a must.

The porcini is found in association with a wide variety of conifers and deciduous trees, including birch, oaks and chestnuts. Depending on conditions (temperature and rain), it is in season from April to May.

IDENTIFICATION

Cap (Fig. 1, i)

The cap is 7–30 centimetres in diameter, starting out as a half-spherical shape before broadening and flattening out at maturity. It is warm brown in colour, fading to off-white at the margins. The cap looks rather dull.

Underside (Fig. 1, iii)

The porcini is part of the *Boletus* group, and so it features sponge-like pores on the underside, at first white in colour, progressing to yellow-brown as the mushroom matures.

Spores

The spores are olive-brown in colour.

Stalk (Fig. 1, ii)

The stalk is off-white, 8–25 centimetres long and up to 7 centimetres wide. It is large in comparison to the cap, and bloated-looking. A characteristic of the species is the textural, net-like pattern (reticulation) visible on the surface of the upper part of the stalk.

Flesh

The flesh is white to off-white, thick and firm.

Fig. 1 *Boletus edulis*

Resources

As you continue your foraging journey, here are some resources you can look to for more information.

Websites

The Australasian Virtual Herbarium <avh.ala.org.au>

Australian Association of Bush Regenerators <aabr.org.au/volunteering/bushcare-and-landcare-volunteering>

Landcare Australia <landcareaustralia.org.au>

Atlas of Living Australia <bie.ala.org.au>

Plants For A Future <pfaf.org>

Food Plants International <foodplantsinternational.com>

Wildfood Store <wildfood.store>

PlantNET <plantnet.rbgsyd.nsw.gov.au>

Cichorieae Portal <cichorieae.e-taxonomy.net>

Botanical.com <botanical.com>

Eatweeds <eatweeds.co.uk>

Weeds Australia <weeds.org.au>

Environmental Weeds of Australia <keyserver.lucidcentral.org/weeds>

Grow Forage Cook Ferment <growforagecookferment.com>

Plant Resources of the World <prota4u.org>

National Centre for Biotechnology Information <ncbi.nlm.nih.gov/Taxonomy>

Encyclopedia of Life <eol.org>

Eat the Weeds <eattheweeds.com>

Edible Wild Food <ediblewildfood.com>

Medicinal Herb Info <medicinalherbinfo.org/000Herbs2016>

Australian Fungi <australianfungi.blogspot.com>

Mushroaming <mushroaming.wordpress.com>

Tall Trees and Mushrooms <morrie2.com>

Selby Shrooms <selbyshrooms.com.au>

Forums

Edible Weeds, Wild Crafting & Foraging in Australia <facebook.com/groups/255804947779277>

Australian Wild Mushroom Hunters <facebook.com/groups/AustralianWildMushroomHunters>

Ebooks

John Henry Clarke, *Materia Medica*, 1902, <materiamedica.info/en/materia-medica/john-henry-clarke/index>.

Joseph A Cocannouer, *Weeds: Guardians of the Soil*, The Devin-Adair Company, Old Greenwich, Connecticut, 1950, <naturalsequencefarming.com/press/Weeds%20guardians%20of%20the%20Soil%20(3).pdf>.

Books

Tim Low, *Wild Food Plants of Australia*, HarperCollins Publishers, Sydney, 1991

Adam Grubb and Annie Raser-Rowland, *The Weed Forager's Handbook*, Hyland House Publishing, Melbourne, 2012.

Ellen Zachos, *Backyard Foraging*, Storey Publishing, North Adams, Massachusetts, 2013.

Peter Latz, *Bushfires & Bushtucker*, IAD Press, Alice Springs, 1995.

Alison Pouliot and Tom May, *Wild Mushrooming*, CSIRO Publishing, Melbourne, 2021.

Genevieve Gates and David Ratkowsky, *A Field Guide to Tasmanian Fungi*, Tasmanian Field Naturalists Club, Hobart, 2014.

FJ Richardson, RG Richardson and RCH Shepherd, *Weeds of the South-East*, 2006.

Luigi Ballerini, *A Feast of Weeds*, University of California Press, Berkeley, California, 2012.

Pat Collins, *The Wondrous World of Weeds*, New Holland, Sydney, 2016.

Pascal Baudar, *The New Wildcrafted Cuisine*, Chelsea Green Publishing, Hartford, Vermont, 2016.

Antonio Carluccio, *Antonio Carluccio Goes Wild*, Headline, London, 2001.

Kirsten Bradley and Nick Ritar, *Milkwood*, Murdoch Books, Sydney, 2018.

AB and JW Cribb, *Wild Food in Australia*, Collins, Sydney, 1974.

Heidi Merika, *Wildcraft*, 2019.

Articles

Jared Diamond, 'The Worst Mistake in the History of the Human Race', *Discover*, May 1987, pp. 64–6.

Dr Max Kwiatkowski, 'Re-creating the Polish "homelandscape": Mushroom hunting in Belanglo', in Elizabeth Drozd and Desmond Cahill (eds), *Polonia in Australia: Challenges and Possibilities in the New Millennium*, Common Ground Publishing, Altona, Vic., 2004.

Notes

p. 14 Slow Food is an organisation that promotes local food and traditional cooking. It was founded by Carlo Petrini in Italy in 1986 and has since spread worldwide.

p. 15 As a practising contemporary artist I have participated in many national and international exhibitions, and received commissions including Food Fight (a C3West commission in partnership with the Museum of Contemporary Art and Liverpool Council, Sydney, 2016); The Rocks Windmill (2013, workshops and public sculpture); Wild Stories (two years of workshops and a solo show, Casula Powerhouse Arts Centre, 2012); and State of the Arts (group exhibition, Italian Pavilion, Venice Biennale 2011).

p. 15 One of my past projects was Wild Food Map (2013–19), a community-driven online platform to identify public-domain food and medicine plants living in the landscape all over the world.

p. 18 Jared Diamond, 'The Worst Mistake in the History of the Human Race', *Discover*, May 1987, pp. 64–6.

p. 19 Authors such as George Monbiot and Tim Ingold are great sources of knowledge regarding the intricate ways in which we relate to place and to other species.

p. 34 Pat Collins, *The Wondrous World of Weeds*, New Holland, Sydney, 2016.

p. 52 Information on the use of *Plantago cunninghamii* and *Plantago debilis* as a food source from Tim Low, *Wild Food Plants of Australia*, HarperCollins Publishers, Sydney, 1991, p. 97.

p. 73 Adam Grubb and Annie Raser-Rowland, *The Weed Forager's Handbook: A Guide to Edible and Medicinal Weeds in Australia*, Hyland House Publishing, Melbourne, 2012.

p. 152 Kirsten Bradley and Nick Ritar, *Milkwood: Real Skills for Down-to-Earth Living*, Murdoch Books, Sydney, 2018.

p. 197 Dr Max Kwiatkowski, 'Re-creating the Polish "homelandscape": Mushroom hunting in Belanglo', in Elizabeth Drozd and Desmond Cahill (eds), *Polonia in Australia: Challenges and Possibilities in the New Millennium*, Common Ground Publishing, Altona, Vic., 2004.

Acknowledgements

This book has its roots in my mother's teachings, the endless patience with which she answered all of my questions about the natural world: why does the spider have eight legs and the fly only six? Why is this a dandelion and this one is not? Why do I need to go harvesting the field mushrooms now? Can't I do it next week?

I truly hope to celebrate her love and respect for all beings, cycles and interconnections through these pages.

From there onwards, as I travelled the world and wondered at some of the most amazing ecologies, I gathered notions and stories from many Elders, experts and free thinkers. I hope that the wisdom you shared is respected in these pages.

A final, heartfelt thank you goes to my collaborators, as you went well beyond what was requested and offered counsel, care for details and consistent availability. Thank you Marnee for the recipes and word wrangling, Hellene for the images, Mirra for the drawings and Diana for the editing; this book is yours as much as mine.

Index

First published in Australia in 2022
by Thames & Hudson Australia Pty Ltd
11 Central Boulevard, Portside Business Park
Port Melbourne, Victoria 3207
ABN: 72 004 751 964

First published in the United Kingdom in 2022
By Thames & Hudson Ltd
181a High Holborn
London WC1V 7QX

First published in the United States of America in 2022
By Thames & Hudson Inc.
500 Fifth Avenue
New York, New York 10110

Eat Weeds © Thames & Hudson Australia 2022

25 24 23 22   5 4 3 2 1

Thames & Hudson Australia wishes to acknowledge that
Aboriginal and Torres Strait Islander people are the first
storytellers of this nation and the traditional custodians of
the land on which we live and work. We acknowledge their
continuing culture and pay respect to Elders past, present
and future.

ISBN 978-1-760-76149-3

ISBN 978-1-760-76279-7 (U.S. edition)

 A catalogue record for this
book is available from the
National Library of Australia

British Library Cataloguing-in-Publication Data
A catalogue record for this book is available from the
British Library

Library of Congress Control Number 2021949146

Every effort has been made to trace accurate ownership
of copyrighted text and visual materials used in this book.
Errors or omissions will be corrected in subsequent editions,
provided notification is sent to the publisher.

Front cover: Hellene Algie, Dandelion *Taraxacum
officinale*, 2021

Photography: Hellene Algie
Illustration: Mirra Whale
Styling and recipes: Marnee Fox
Design: Ashlea O'Neill, Salt Camp Studio
Editing: Diana Hill
Printed and bound in China by 1010 Printing
International Limited

Be the first to know about our new releases,
exclusive content and author events by visiting

thamesandhudson.com.au
thamesandhudson.com
thamesandhudsonusa.com

FSC® is dedicated to the promotion of responsible forest
management worldwide. This book is made of material from
FSC®-certified forests and other controlled sources.

MIX
Paper from
responsible sources
FSC® C016973

Sea continued

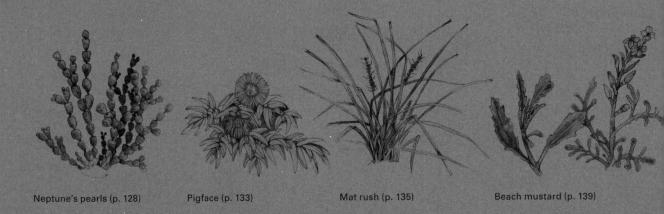

Neptune's pearls (p. 128)

Pigface (p. 133)

Mat rush (p. 135)

Beach mustard (p. 139)

Wild fennel (p. 159)

Native spinach (p. 162)

Cobbler's pegs (p. 166)

Dock (p. 169)

Chapter 05
—
Forest

P. 188

Cleavers (p. 186)

Saffron milk cap (p. 199)

Slippery Jack (p. 202)